This book is an incredible resource for anyone trying to grow or step into a healthier and more life-giving marriage. Aaron and Jen pull no punches; are honest, raw, and authentic; and show that a marriage in pursuit of Jesus can change the world.

JEFFERSON BETHKE, *NEW YORK TIMES* BESTSELLING
AUTHOR OF *JESUS > RELIGION*

In these pages Aaron and Jen have fantastically conveyed the purpose of the mission and meaning of marriage. A powerful read that left us both inspired and awed that we get to participate in something so powerful—marriage— and designed and created by a mighty God for an amazing adventure. No doubt this will become a must-read for decades to come!

JEREMY AND AUDREY ROLOFF, AUTHORS OF *A LOVE LETTER LIFE*, FOUNDERS OF BEATING 50 PERCENT

There is a short list of books I'm stashing away for my three small kiddos to read when they are older—*Marriage After God* is one of them. Dear couples of the world, you have picked up a treasure! This book will give you clear direction to live out God's will for your marriage. There is no greater gift you can give yourselves than to run after Him together. *Marriage After God* will show you how!

LARA CASEY, AUTHOR OF *CULTIVATE* AND *MAKE IT HAPPEN*

Marriage After God is *not* your typical marriage book. Rather than focus on the common symptoms of marriage dysfunction and lack of intimacy, *Marriage After God* dives into and focuses on the root issues: the need for faith, biblical truth, fellowship, ministry and God-ordained vision. The Smiths take the wise path of urging us to grow a better marriage by focusing first on growing closer to God.

GARY THOMAS

In *Marriage After God*, you will discover how to grab your spouse's hand and chase your calling together—one that will be both deeply satisfying as well as God-glorifying. Using uncommon transparency, Aaron and Jennifer give you a backstage view of their marriage, sharing lessons they have learned that will in turn inspire you to pursue your own unique purpose as a couple. A fabulous book to study together to strengthen your marriage as you deepen your faith.

KAREN EHMAN, *NEW YORK TIMES* BESTSELLING AUTHOR OF *KEEP SHOWING UP*, FIRST 5 APP BIBLE TEACHER, PROVERBS 31 MINISTRIES SPEAKER, WIFE, AND MOTHER OF THREE

Marriage is hard. We need people who are brave enough to share honestly about the challenges couples face as they try and live out a marriage after God. That's exactly what Aaron and Jennifer do in this book. They share their story, but even more, they point us back toward the bigger story of God and the truth of His Word.

JERRAD LOPES, HOST OF THE *DAD TIRED* PODCAST

Aaron and Jennifer Smith know from experience that a marriage wholeheartedly dedicated to God is a powerful thing. And if couples fight to remain unified, devoted to God and His purposes, the impact of such a bond can be incredibly influential for the kingdom. Prepare your heart to be encouraged and generously equipped as this book will challenge you not only to hear God's Word, but to trust it, believe it, and put it into action.

ANNE-RENEE GUMLEY, COAUTHOR OF *SHINY THINGS*, COHOST OF THE *ALL THE MOM THINGS* PODCAST

The Smiths possess a wisdom that has been hard-won as a married couple. I respect them deeply for how they have taken what they've been learning and present it to the rest of us wrapped in so much truth and grace. *Marriage After God* helps create stronger marriage relationships while urging couples to honor God above all else. It's an amazing resource!

AMANDA BACON, PROVERBS 31 MINISTRIES, AUTHOR OF *SHINY THINGS*, COHOST OF THE *ALL THE MOM THINGS* PODCAST

In *Marriage After God*, Aaron and Jennifer Smith have laid out an easy-to-read and easy-to-follow plan for both husband and wife to work together to create an extraordinary marriage. With their love for one another and for the reader, combined with their signature transparency, this book is a must-read for every couple.

TONY AND ALISA DILORENZO, COFOUNDERS OF ONE EXTRAORDINARY MARRIAGE

Marriage After God is an emboldening guide to building a life of love on an unshakable foundation. No matter where you find yourself as a couple today, you will find a refreshing vulnerability and a resolute hope from Aaron and Jennifer in these pages. A must-read for every couple!

PATRICK AND RUTH SCHWENK, COFOUNDERS
OF THEBETTERLIFEMINISTRY.COM, COAUTHORS
OF *FOR BETTER OR FOR KIDS*

In a culture confused by too many differing messages, traditional marriage has been brought into question. This important book will give guidance and inspiration for the profound purpose of marriage and the way to pursue a strong partnership that will last a lifetime. Compassion and wisdom in each page will inspire all who desire to grow stronger in their marriage.

SALLY CLARKSON, AUTHOR, SPEAKER, PODCASTER AND BLOGGER

Marriage After God is a powerful resource of truth that is needed now more than ever. Aaron and Jennifer Smith have done an incredible job of bringing biblical truths about marriage to a practical application. You will be blessed by their transparency, wisdom, and personal story of God's redeeming power. I can't wait to see how God uses this book to bring unity, hope, and healing to all who read it!

KATIE FARRELL, AUTHOR OF THE *DASHING DISH* COOKBOOK,
DEVOTIONS FOR A HEALTHIER YOU, AND *NOURISH*

Every couple should read this book. It will help them discover God's blueprint for their marriage! In *Marriage After God*, Aaron and Jen teach the core elements of biblical marriage and challenge every couple to evaluate whether their perspective of their own marriage is founded on God's purposes by taking inventory of their gifts, talents, and experiences so that they can fulfill the unique purposes God has designed for them.

ISAAC AND ANGIE TOLPIN, HOSTS OF THE *COURAGEOUS
PARENTING* PODCAST, AUTHOR OF *REDEEMING CHILDBIRTH*,
AND FOUNDER OF COURAGEOUS MOM MINISTRIES

In *Marriage After God*, Aaron and Jennifer Smith have boiled the complexity of a godly marriage down to its essential nuggets. This book is honest, straightforward, biblical, and a great tool for any couple that aims to honor God in the midst of real life.

DR. JULI SLATTERY, PSYCHOLOGIST, AUTHOR
OF *RETHINKING SEXUALITY*

Aaron and Jennifer Smith have written a book packed full of Scripture and admonishments that encourage unity. A book for *all* marriages, it offers direction while boldly submitting your marriage before God, to honor, pursue and experience His sacred marital design. You'll be sure to walk away with a biblical understanding and excitement to pursue God's plans and purposes in your very own marriage.

CODY AND STACY MEHAN

As a young wife, I heard a truth that has never left me: "The closer you draw to God, the closer you'll be able to draw to your spouse." *Marriage After God* is a beautiful testimony to this truth. I'm thankful for Aaron and Jennifer's message of striving for an extraordinary marriage with God at the center. This book is perfect for couples who want to be stronger together and impact the world in amazing ways!

TRICIA GOYER, *USA TODAY* BESTSELLING AUTHOR OF
OVER SEVENTY BOOKS, INCLUDING *WALK IT OUT*

We need more couples like Aaron and Jennifer! These two are doing a wonderful job of leading the charge and showing us how to live out God's amazing purpose for marriage, a purpose that is so much bigger than simply achieving a happily-ever-after. Their new book *Marriage After God* shows the importance of chasing hard after God while using your marriage to glorify Him.

KRISTEN CLARK AND BETHANY BEAL, COFOUNDERS
OF GIRLDEFINED MINISTRIES, AUTHORS OF *SEX,
PURITY, AND THE LONGINGS OF A GIRL'S HEART*

An extraordinary marriage is available to you. Your first step is to say yes to opening and reading what Aaron and Jennifer say in this book. We highly recommend it!

JACKIE AND STEPHANA BLEDSOE, AUTHORS, SPEAKERS,
FOUNDERS OF *HAPPILYMARRIEDCOUPLES.COM*

MARRIAGE
AFTER GOD

*Chasing Boldly After God's
Purpose for Your Life Together*

Aaron & Jennifer Smith

ZONDERVAN

Marriage After God
Copyright © 2019 by Aaron Smith and Jennifer Smith

ISBN 978-0-310-35533-5 (hardcover)

ISBN 978-0-310-35536-6 (audio)

ISBN 978-0-310-35535-9 (ebook)

Requests for information should be addressed to:
Zondervan, *3900 Sparks Dr. SE, Grand Rapids, Michigan 49546*

Authors are represented by The Christopher Ferebee Agency, www .christopherferebee.com.

Art direction: James W. Hall IV
Cover photo: © layritten/iStock
Interior design: Denise Froehlich

Printed in the United States of America

19 20 21 22 23 /LSC/ 10 9 8 7 6 5 4 3 2 1

To every married couple who faithfully lives out what it means to be a marriage after God. Thank you for your obedience to the Scriptures and for showing the rest of the world a picture of the true gospel through the way you intentionally live your lives for our King!

CONTENTS

FOREWORD

Aaron and Jennifer Smith have found something every couple hopes to find but few do—an excellent marriage. This couple is the real deal. The Smiths aren't sharing some theory they believe is true. They are living the message of this book.

Aaron and Jennifer really do have a marriage that is built on following hard after God—evidenced by the love they have for each other; the peace in their home; their happy, obedient children; and their fruitfulness in ministry. This couple has been proven in the crucible of discipleship. They genuinely and consistently embody the teaching they share with others.

You are about to experience their open, raw, honest, authentic journey to a biblically-mature marriage and the best that God intended for them. The real heart of this book, however, is its message for the Christian church—its message for *your* marriage.

Did God intend more for Christian marriage than that a couple enjoy each other through life?

As wonderful as a great marriage can be, *Marriage After God* teaches that God created your marriage for far more than most Christian couples ever realize. Your marriage is for His purpose, not yours. Have you discovered everything God intended for your marriage? Do you know what that purpose is? Keep reading . . . you're about to find out! And in the process, you'll grow closer than ever before in the most important relationship you'll ever have, this side of heaven.

Matt and Lisa Jacobson

Authors of *100 Ways to Love Your Wife*
and *100 Ways to Love Your Husband*

INTRODUCTION

What if I told you that your marriage has a purpose far beyond happily ever after? What if I told you that the unity between you and your spouse was created for something extraordinary?

God, your Creator and your Savior, has created you and your spouse with complete and perfect thoughtfulness. God, your provider and your Heavenly Father, has unlimited resources and immeasurable creativity. God, who is patient and loving, is pursuing you and your spouse every single day, inviting you to participate in the extraordinary things He is already doing.

Do you believe God wants more for your life and marriage, just as you do? Do you believe God wants more for your marriage than for you to just make each other happy? Do you believe God can do anything—move mountains, open doors, and part seas to get you to the place where He wants you the most?

Belief is powerful. Belief propels people from a place of dreaming to a place of doing. Belief in God is confidence and trust in Him. Believing God made you and your marriage with great purpose is the beginning of an incredible adventure you will never regret.

BELIEF propels people from a place of **DREAMING** to a place of **DOING.**

When Jennifer and I considered what spurred us toward a desire to serve God together, we agreed that it was our belief that God could and would use us as a team for His glory. And that belief gave us the courage to say yes to Him over and over and over again. Even and especially during the hard times in our story.

We said yes to God when we decided to stay together, when it felt easier to walk away. We said yes to God when we chose to love each other, even when we didn't feel so in love. We said yes to obeying His Word when we did everything we could to get out of debt. We said yes to God when He showed us ways we could serve His body, and we said yes to God when He invited us to share our story. Not all of our "yeses" to God were easy; however, our mutual desire to please God is what helped us to say yes and to persevere.

When Jennifer and I got married, we had a united desire to serve God together. We didn't know exactly what it would look like, but we were willing to explore the opportunities He had for us as a married couple. Throughout our time of dating and being engaged, we prayed we would have an extraordinary marriage. However, we didn't stop there. We didn't only ask God for an extraordinary marriage; we also prayed God would use our marriage to do extraordinary things to build His kingdom.

Since we said "I do" and committed our marriage to the Lord, we have been on a journey of saying yes to God, a journey we both agree has been quite extraordinary. Not only because of the experiences we have had or the accomplishments we have reached, but because God is extraordinary. And He longs to bring His extraordinary into our lives. He is the reason we have been able to endure this journey together. We have experienced both poverty and abundance; we have traveled to different parts of the world as missionaries motivated to share the gospel with others; we have started businesses and ministries; we have overcome destructive sin patterns; we have grown our family size, intentionally striving to leave a legacy with our children; and we continue to participate in God's plan for our lives as He invites us to do all that He prepared for us to do, together. But it is all because of God. He gets the glory in our lives.

Our journey has not been void of the enemy's attacks to thwart God's purpose for our marriage. In fact, the enemy's flaming arrows, in combination with our own sin, almost destroyed our marriage. Pornography addiction, emotional eating, irrational jealousy, foolishness, and constant battles of selfishness and pride have all been difficult areas of our marriage that we have had to battle. The hardships we have encountered in marriage have been painful. We have often wrestled with doubt and insecurities about our relationship with each other and with God. Yet, no matter what we have faced, and no matter what we will face in the future, we continue to pray that God will give us an extraordinary marriage and that He will use our marriage for His extraordinary purposes.

In 2011, Jennifer and I launched our online marriage ministries (HusbandRevolution.com and UnveiledWife.com) to share with husbands and wives what God was teaching us about marriage. When we began these ministries, we had no idea what they would become. Motivated by a perspective that our lives are a ministry for God to work through, we said yes to God when He invited us to share our story with the world in a way we were already familiar with, *blogging*. Through these two sites we share daily marriage prayers, encouragement, biblical teaching on faith and marriage, date night ideas, and reviews of Christian books and movies. We share personal stories of what we have experienced in our own marriage and how God continues to transform us into the husband and wife He created us to be. Since the first day we created these ministries, our desire has been to encourage married couples to turn their hearts toward God and trust in Him with their marriage. With the few tools we had in our tool belt, we got started, and this adventure quickly grew into an unimaginable reach into the hearts and homes of couples all around the world.

With the influence we were gaining in the lives of other married couples, we asked the Lord to use us to encourage them to be biblical men and women. We were confident that if we could inspire them and challenge them to be people who read God's Word and desire His will for their lives, then God would move in these marriages and use them for the marvelous work He desires His people to do. We imagined hundreds of thousands of strong, thriving marriages reflecting God's love story and impacting the lives of others as they faithfully live out all that God has called them to. We envisioned husbands and wives being unified in their relationship and in their parenting, full of joy and contentment. We could see communities being blessed by the lives and examples of these couples. We could see relationships being healed, needs being met, talents being used, businesses and ministries being started, and the lost being saved because husbands and wives said yes to God, working together to build His kingdom.

Eager to see husbands and wives embrace what God has for them, we wondered how we could inspire them to start considering the purpose of their marriage and help guide them to set the foundation necessary to fulfill that purpose. We wanted to point them to the Word of God and prompt them to answer some challenging questions. We felt led to write two devotionals that would lead a husband and wife through God's Word and invite them to consider how they can actively pursue an extraordinary, God-centered marriage. So we coauthored and self-published *Husband After God* and *Wife After God,* thirty-day devotionals that have been read by thousands of men and women.

Not long after publishing our devotionals, we began to receive messages from couples asking what they could read next to encourage them on their marriage journey. So we began to consider what resource we could provide next to inspire husbands and wives to continue chasing after God. This is the seed that would grow into the message of *Marriage After God.* We knew God wanted more couples to pray the same prayer we have been praying and to experience His extraordinary purposes for their lives. Yet, we believe it was also a message God wanted us to experience in our marriage for ourselves. He wanted us to mature in our relationship with each other and with Him.

We wouldn't say we are done experiencing what it means to have a marriage after God. In reality, this will be a message we will continue to live out and pursue until Christ returns or we are called home. However, God has given us an incredible opportunity to present this message to others through this book, to inspire husbands and wives who want to chase after Him and to do His will together, and we are eager to see how God uses this book to do His work in all of our lives.

A marriage after God is an extraordinary journey of making ourselves known to God, knowing God, and being willing to let Him use our marriages for His purposes. A marriage after God is one that can faithfully say what the people of Israel said in Exodus 19:8, "All that the LORD has spoken we will do." *Happily ever after* is a nice thought and a good thing to hope for, but it should not be your end goal. There is an amazing purpose for your marriage, more than just making each other happy. We desire you to pursue kingdom purposes with your marriage, to be a testimony to others of God's love and amazing grace.

This world we live in has been tainted by darkness, but you are called to be the light of the world! It is you and your marriage that should be the light people long to experience. But you cannot be a light for others if you are allowing your marriage to be overrun by darkness. Those who belong to God have been created for so much more! You have been created for so much more! And your spouse has been created for so much more!

Our vision for this book is to get you and your spouse excited about using your marriage for God! We desire that you two experience the incredible intimacy of unity as you boldly chase after God's will and purpose for your marriage.

This book is for the marriages who are ready to finally see what God brought them together for. Maybe you and your spouse have been having conversations about what is next, what you should be investing in, or how you can be used by God to effectively fulfill the purpose He created you for, the purpose He brought you together for. You have been in a great place in your marriage and with God, but there is a tugging on your heart to do something more. You picked up this book because you don't want to be stagnant; you want to experience the extraordinary! Our hope and prayer is that this book takes you on a journey of discovery, inspiration, and affirmation as God invites you to work together as a team for His glory.

If you and your spouse are in a different place, a broken place where you are barely hanging on, our hope is that this book would be the very thing to convince you to turn your heart back toward God and have the courage to change your perspective of your spouse and your marriage. Maybe it will be the very thing your marriage needs, to push you closer to the only One who can help you put it back in order.

So, we welcome you, no matter what condition your marriage is currently in, and we challenge you to take this adventure with us to commit your marriage to God and see how He moves in your life, your spouse's life, and the many other lives He will impact because you were willing to say yes to Him.

Everything begins with a first step; reading this book is your first step. We pray it won't be long before you and your spouse are running, with your hearts aligned with God's, toward the extraordinary good work God has already prepared for you to do.

You were created for this. Ephesians 2:10 confirms this, declaring, "For we are his workmanship, created in Christ Jesus for good works, which God prepared beforehand, that we should walk in them." You and your spouse were made by God, and your marriage relationship was designed by Him to do good works for His name's sake, works that He had in mind long before you were created. You can believe this truth and so be empowered to walk in the extraordinary purpose you have been uniquely created by God to do.

OUR PRAYER FOR THE COUPLE READING THIS BOOK

Dear Lord,

We pray for the husband and wife reading this book. May Your Holy Spirit use this book to inspire their hearts to boldly chase after You and say yes to the extraordinary invitations You have prepared for them. We pray this couple will grow in their understanding of the power and purpose of their marriage. Reveal to them the specific plans You have for them. We pray You would use this marriage to do incredible work to build Your kingdom. In this dark world, may You protect this couple from the attacks of the enemy. May You cleanse them from sin and continue to shape them into the husband and wife You created them to be. May they realize they bear Your image and that they are a light in this world and a beacon of hope to the lost and lonely. We ask You to guide this couple and unite them as a team to carry out the unique purposes You have for them in Jesus's name.

Amen!

Part 1

WHAT IS A MARRIAGE AFTER GOD?
THE DEFINITION

Chapter 1

GOD'S PURPOSE
FOR MARRIAGE

D usk draped across the mountainous landscape, framed by an elegant floor-to-ceiling window. The snow-capped peaks above and the rushing river below created a peaceful backdrop for the opening session of our very first Marriage After God Gathering. I (Jennifer) stood at the large window of the rustic lodge we had rented for this special event and gazed at the wonder of God's creation, my heart filled with gratitude for this opportunity.

For six long months, Aaron and I had prayed and prepared for this gathering and the couples who would attend. We had considered every detail of the event: hand-picking the venue, hiring a chef, and designing study guides for each participant. Although many people might call this event a retreat, Aaron and I felt strongly that it needed to be called something special. Hoping it would be an experience of closeness and camaraderie, we called it a gathering. To us this felt more unifying, more intimate, more intentional. There was still plenty of time to retreat, reflect, and be refreshed; however, that was not the primary purpose of *this* marriage gathering. We wanted couples who were seeking God's will for their lives and marriages, couples wondering and praying, "God, what's next? What can our marriage do for You?"

Buzzing with anticipation, eleven couples gathered with us in the living room to begin our first session. These eleven couples represented a beautiful diversity of marriages. Some had celebrated many faithful years together, while others had just begun their journey as one. Some had children, while others did not. Some were already in the midst of pursuing ministry together, while others were dreaming about what they could do as a team for God. All different types of people with different experiences, gifts, passions, and resources, yet as a group, we were all unified in one mission, one mind, and one heart. Our sole desire was to honor God with what He had given to us. Each couple sitting around the living room that evening recognized the power of God in their lives, and they were sure God had even more for their marriages, a purpose that would have an unfathomable impact in the world.

Aaron and I didn't know exactly how the gathering would turn out because we had never done anything like this before, but we said yes to God in faith that this vision was planted in our hearts by Him, and we couldn't wait to see it fulfilled.

I (Aaron) felt strongly that we should not shy away from teaching on sensitive marriage topics such as intimacy, finances, and the importance of community. The more we worked on the curriculum for this gathering, the more enthusiastic we became. But as we planned, the ever-looming question we had to answer was: *How are we going to open this gathering?* Soon the answer became clear. We had to start with the Bible.

No other topic we could teach on made sense, nor would any of the other topics matter, if we neglected to start with the Bible. We felt this urge first and foremost to encourage every couple to persevere as faithful men and women who are led according to the truth of God's Word. We knew from our own experience of pursuing ministry as a team for God that laying the foundation for the importance of God's Word in our lives is crucial. We knew we had to start there.

That gathering and those couples were the catalyst for this book. The message we opened up with during that first session is the very same message we are going to open up this book with, because without it nothing else we shared with them, and what we are about to share with you, will matter at all. Chasing boldly after God's purpose for your life together, understanding that purpose, and fulfilling that purpose is all a result of knowing God and submitting to Him in reverence. A marriage after God is a husband and wife who are obedient to fulfill all that God has called them to.

As husbands and wives who desire to walk in God's will and His ways, we must be, above all else, men and women *of the Word*.

Men and Women of the Word

It is God's Word and His Word alone that we, as faithful men and women, stand on. In fact, without the Bible, there can be no faith, salvation, maturity, wisdom, or knowledge of the Holy One, let alone a *marriage after God*. The Bible is and must always remain our only source for defining what our lives and marriages mean and what they are meant for. God gave us His Word because He knew that His ideas, especially His creation of marriage, would be attacked from the very beginning. He knew that our hearts would be prone to wander far from His ideas and His ways. He knew that His enemy, and ours, would desire to destroy the very idea of marriage, doing anything and everything he could do to denigrate its meaning and purpose. Therefore, as the perfect Creator, God gave us His manual for life. It is up to us to make the choice to follow it, walking out our faith through obedience, regardless of the resistance we encounter from our flesh and from our enemy.

From the very beginning, the enemy was at work deceiving and confusing man with a simple question, "Did God actually say . . . ?" (Genesis 3:1), and he hasn't changed his strategy. This enemy of ours has only come to steal and kill and destroy, and he is still at work doing this by convincing husbands and wives to ask the very same question, "Did God actually say . . . ?" This question has been hissed so many times now into the ears and hearts of husbands and wives that the Word of God is just not as important to them as it should be; it is no longer the authority of their lives. Instead, they doubt the Bible and question its message. The enemy knows that if God's people don't believe or trust what God has said, then they will not read what He has said. And if God's people do not read His Word or trust it, then why would they obey it? Let us not be deceived by the enemy or deceived by our flesh. Instead, let us heed the words in James 1:22, "But be doers of the word, and not hearers only, deceiving yourselves."

Ignoring, doubting, or disobeying God's Word has led many marriages to confusion, suffering, abuse, alienation, division, or divorce. In contrast, couples who hear God's Word, believe it, and put it into action will become a light shining in the darkness, an example to others of a worthy path to take (see Psalm 119:105).

Before we start to talk about how the Bible defines us and our marriages, before we encourage you to use your marriage for God's purposes, and before we talk about what it actually looks like to have a marriage that is being used by God for kingdom work, ask yourself what you believe about His Word. Everything we are discussing in this book is drenched in Scripture and biblical principles. The Bible is the basis of our faith. It is the very substance of what we claim to believe. It is the foundation of our life. As Jesus reminds us, "Everyone then who hears these words of mine and does them will be like a wise man who built his house on the rock" (Matthew 7:24). Let us then build our marriages on a solid foundation that is found only in the truth of God's Word.

So, we would like to ask you, what is your relationship with the Bible? We want you to take a moment to consider and discuss this question with your spouse, and then continue reading.

What the Bible Says about Marriage

So then, what does the Bible say about marriage? Why did God create this beautifully messy thing called holy matrimony?

Paul proclaimed, "For [God's] invisible attributes, namely, his eternal power and divine nature, have been clearly perceived, ever since the creation of the world, in the things that have been made" (Romans 1:20). God made everything to show the world who He is and what kind of God He is. Every star, every plant, each and every animal, every cell, light, wind, and sound, it was all created with this purpose in mind. Marriage, too, is something that God created to reveal His nature. Marriage is not man's idea, nor is it anything man could ever define. Marriage is a heavenly concept with divine implications.

Marriage was so important, in fact, that God didn't waste a moment to introduce this powerful symbol to us. Right in the very beginning of the Bible, not more than twenty-six verses in and barely six days into history, God chose to unveil His divine masterpiece: "Then God said, 'Let us make man in our image, after our likeness. And let them have dominion over the fish of the sea and over the birds of the heavens and over the livestock and over all the earth and over every creeping thing that creeps on the earth.' So God created man in his own image, in the image of God he created him; male and female he created them" (Genesis 1:26–27).

After God creates Eve, and after Adam rejoices in his new companion, the Bible states in Genesis 2:24: "Therefore a man shall leave his father and his mother and hold fast to his wife, and they shall become one flesh."

Marriage isn't simply a part of God's perfect creation; it was a gift He gave to His favorite part of creation—man and woman. In fact, everything God created was for the benefit of the man and the woman. He gave it all to them for food, for pleasure, to cultivate, subdue, and rule over. On almost every day of creation, God declared his work to be "good" (Genesis 1:10, 18, 21, 25). But after He created man and woman, he declared it all to be *very* good (Genesis 1:31). Do you see it? Are you beginning to grasp His grand narrative? Creation was only good until the introduction of man and woman made it *very* good. Doesn't this show us just how much God values and cares for His children, how much He values and cares for you, and how much He values your marriage?

Humanity is God's greatest creation, and His desire is to show us who He is. God's decision to bring man and woman together in marriage wasn't an afterthought, although it can seem that way when we read about Adam not seeing a suitable helper out of all the animals he was naming. On the contrary, marriage, Adam and Eve being united, was necessary for God's purposes to be fulfilled. God had a job for his two new children to fulfill, and their marriage was the vehicle to accomplish that job. This job He had for them was simple, yet also profoundly mysterious. Simple in that they were told to tend to the garden and be fruitful and multiply, profoundly mysterious in that ultimately their marriage would be a picture of Christ and the church. Paul points this out in Ephesians 5:31–32, where he reiterates the words of Genesis and pushes the symbol farther: "'Therefore a man shall leave his father and mother and hold fast to his wife, and the two shall become one flesh.' This mystery is profound, and I am saying that it refers to Christ and the church." In God's infinite creativity and wisdom, He used marriage to masterfully paint for all the world a picture of His love and His redemption plan.

As we reflect on the words of Paul, we can begin to see God's divine purpose for marriage. Marriage is much more than an earthly institution. It is not just a man and a woman coming together under the same roof with a legal document stating that the state recognizes this to be the case. Marriage is and always will be an earthly symbol of a heavenly truth. Marriage is a picture of Christ and His relationship with the church. This is what God created marriage for. The symbol of unity within marriage has a greater purpose to serve than a husband and wife coming together for their own satisfaction or desire. The relationship between a husband and wife, when they operate in obedience to

MARRIAGE is and always will be an earthly symbol of a heavenly TRUTH.

God's Word, is the representation and reflection of the gospel, the redemption of man being reconciled through Christ to God.

God reinforces the power of unity within marriage again and again throughout His Word by telling us that a husband and wife are one flesh. Genesis 2:24, Matthew 19:5, Mark 10:8, and Ephesians 5:31 all show us that marriage is the spiritual event of two separate creatures becoming one, or in other words, an entirely "new creation." This new creation teaches us and the world that God's plan for humanity is to make them one with His Son in an inseparable unity. What a wonderful and powerful way to show the ones He loves that "neither death, nor life, nor angels, nor principalities, nor powers, nor things present, nor things to come, nor height, nor depth, nor any other creature, shall be able to separate us from the love of God, which is in Christ Jesus our Lord" (Romans 8:38–39 KJV).

This new creation that a marriage creates, when two become one, is to show the world the supremely freeing truth that "if anyone is in Christ, he is a new creation. The old has passed away; behold, the new has come" (2 Corinthians 5:17).

As the author in Song of Solomon expresses his love for his bride in Song of Solomon 8:7, he makes a bold statement, in essence that love cannot be purchased. The love you choose to walk in, in your marriage, is meant to show the world this same truth—that God's love is unearned and cannot be bought with anything you have to offer.

Our marriages are to be walking examples of God's unending love, grace, and mercy. Whether we are being good examples, walking in the direction and command of the Lord, or we are being disobedient and rebellious to it, we are being a symbol to the world. What gospel is your marriage preaching to this lost

Your marriage is God's, and He desires for it to be done HIS WAY and for HIS PURPOSES!

and dying world? Is it proclaiming the never-ending and ever-patient love of God?

Our marriages can and should bring glory to God and point outsiders, who are looking in, to a loving and redeeming God. Marriage was created by God, it is His, and He desires for it to be used His way and for His purposes. More to the point: Your marriage is God's, and He desires for it to be done His way and for His purposes!

Are you ready for that?

QUESTIONS FOR REFLECTION

1. How would you define your relationship with the Bible, both individually and as a couple?
2. According to Scripture, what is the purpose of marriage?
3. How does your marriage reflect the love of Christ for His bride, the church? How does it fall short of reflecting that divine love?

Chapter 2

THE WAR ON YOUR
EFFECTIVENESS

What if we told you that the first and greatest ministry you and your spouse will do together is the ministry you have in your own marriage? That's right! Your marriage itself *is* ministry! Even before you and your spouse ever do any work together to build God's kingdom outside of your relationship, the most necessary ministry you will participate in must first be experienced and fulfilled in your own marriage.

You are already in ministry as you seek to bless, support, and meet the needs of one another. Your marriage is a gift, given to you by God. How you receive this gift and how you treat it matters. As you minister to your spouse, motivated by the love of God, you will be effectively directing their heart toward the Lord. And as you and your spouse live out the true gospel toward each other, then you simultaneously will be effective in sharing God's gospel with the rest of the world as your marriage reflects His goodness, love, and amazing grace.

Adam and Eve were the first people to experience the gift of marriage. They were the first husband and wife to experience the power of unity in marriage, and yet it didn't take very long for the enemy to declare war on them. Satan saw right away the impact a husband and wife can make when they are unified as one and are devoted to following God. He understood the impact they could make in effectively building God's kingdom. So he did not waste any time in deceiving man and woman, and he hasn't slowed down at all since that dark day when sin entered the world.

Satan knew marriage was important to God, so he sought to destroy Adam and Eve's effectiveness and any purpose God had for them. He sought to destroy their relationship with God and with each other. In the garden that day when he tempted Eve, he began a war that continues to be fought today—a war on our effectiveness. The enemy is convinced that if he can stop or destroy a marriage after God, then he can stop the effectiveness God can have in this world.

Attacks on Our Marriage

Our marriage has not been exempt from this war. Over the years there have been many attempts by the enemy to destroy our marriage and stop the ministry we were trying to pursue. Whether it was temptations of the flesh, conflict with other family members, naysayers who disagreed with our message online, or physical circumstances that burdened our hearts and added stress to our relationship, we have experienced time and again the temptation the enemy has dangled in front of us to chase after anything *but* what God has desired for us. When we are tempted to sin, to

Our marriage relationship has an **IMPACT** no matter where we are or what we are doing.

doubt, to reject God's invitation to carry out His will, we are self-focused, and the effectiveness of our marriage decreases. And if we can't minister to each other in marriage, we definitely won't have what it takes to minister to others.

For example, I (Jennifer) remember a time when a silly argument got in the way of our ministry. Aaron and I were shopping at a grocery store, arguing as we went up and down the aisles putting items we needed into a small cart. It wasn't a heated argument, but our disagreement was obvious nonetheless. The tones we used and the body language alone spoke volumes.

Later that evening, I jumped on social media and a woman had left a comment that she had seen us in the store that day and just wanted to say hello. Although she said nothing about how we had behaved, I was embarrassed at what she may have witnessed. My heart also ached for how I had responded to my husband in the store, for his sake. I was not caring for him in that moment. This was one of the first times I realized that our marriage relationship has an impact no matter where we are or what we are doing. This argument we had in the grocery store not only disrupted our unity, but it definitely did not reflect the love story of God to others around us. The enemy loves it when we destroy our own effectiveness because of selfishness and pride. He loves it when we are so consumed with ourselves that we miss the opportunity to serve both our spouse and others.

Another memory that is seared into my (Aaron's) heart occurred seven years into our marriage. Jennifer and I were standing in our tiny kitchen, arguing loudly, each trying desperately to be heard and proven right. Meanwhile, our eighteen-month-old son Eliott stood between us, crying. His cries couldn't match our volume, although it added to the noise. How long he stood there crying we don't know, but when we finally heard him, we stopped arguing immediately. That moment was an eye-opener for us, reminding us of the impact we have in the lives of our children. There is no way a child can feel safe and secure when his parents are at odds with each other, when the atmosphere in the home is angry and chaotic. It is our responsibility to be the light of Christ and teach our children who God is through our words and our actions. We realized that if we were not united in our relationship, we would not be able to love and disciple our children effectively.

This is what we have experienced and endured over our years of marriage, and we bet you and your spouse have encountered this same battle. This war is one we cannot ignore or overlook; rather, we need to be prepared to defend this gift of marriage and able to fulfill the purpose God has for us, the purpose the enemy is terrified to see us fulfill. It's one thing to decide that you are going to step out in faith and do something great for God. It's an entirely different thing to try and do so with nonstop opposition from an enemy.

The Example of Nehemiah

Nehemiah, a cupbearer to King Artaxerxes in the fifth century BC, understood this war all too well. His heart broke when he learned that the walls of his beloved Jerusalem were in ruins and his fellow Israelites were left unprotected. He knew he had to do something about the situation. After much prayer, he sought the permission and blessing of the king to evaluate and repair the wall, and the king agreed. What a colossal task! But Nehemiah had a clear mission, and he recognized that God's hand was clearly upon him, giving him all the resources and credentials he needed to accomplish the task (Nehemiah 2:8).

Nehemiah believed God had called him and equipped him to do this work—and just like that, the wall was repaired, everything went smoothly, and nothing ever hindered Nehemiah from doing this work. At least this is how we hope things would go for him, and for us when we chase after God's plan for our lives, but we all know this is not the case. The moment anyone steps out in faith to make waves for the kingdom of heaven, we can guarantee there will be opposition.

Nehemiah came into opposition the moment he stepped foot on the soil of God's chosen people. His enemies had one goal, to stop Nehemiah from finishing the work set before him by God. They started by jeering at him and getting him to question whether what he was doing was good and right, saying, "What is this thing that you are doing? Are you rebelling against the king?" (Nehemiah 2:19).

If the enemy can get you to question the things that you know to be true, then he can get you to doubt what you are doing. But instead of stopping the work, Nehemiah pushed forward. He gathered all the people together and began rebuilding the city walls. One brick, two bricks, a thousand bricks, a gate, a second gate, one stone upon another, working hard to fulfill the purpose God placed in his heart.

Jesus warns us too of the opposition we will encounter in this life. "If they persecuted me, they will also persecute you" (John 15:20), he declared. We have a real enemy that wants nothing more than to disrupt, dismantle, disorganize, and discombobulate, if not destroy, the effectiveness of our marriage. For this reason, Peter exhorts us, "Be sober-minded; be watchful. Your adversary the devil prowls around like a roaring lion, seeking someone to devour" (1 Peter 5:8).

Being aware of the enemy's tactics is crucial. As you continue walking with the Lord, don't doubt the good you are doing in your marriage, and don't ever stop the ministry of loving your spouse, so that you will not be made ineffective in your ministry. Whether you are in the grocery store or the kitchen, no matter what it is you are doing, your marriage has the power to build one another up. Either your marriage will radiate the gospel in everything you do and say or it will be a source of contention and conflict for you and for others. The choice is yours, expressed in every place through your every action, great and small.

As you and your spouse take your first steps on the soil of extraordinary, and as you begin to pick up and stack the bricks of obedience, you will need to be prepared to defend against the enemy, because he will try to stop you. He will do everything he can to try and steal your effectiveness and impact in this world.

This is not a mandate for perfection, but an exhortation for protection. If we know the strategy and tactics of our enemy, we can protect our marriages and our effectiveness for God. So here we will examine five tactics the enemy employs to reduce our effectiveness as a couple.

Five Tactics of the Enemy

1. FEAR

What you fear has the most power in your life. If you fear man, then man and his ideas and opinions about you are going to dictate your effectiveness. If you fear failure, then you will never try anything you "might" fail at. The devil wants you to be afraid of what lies ahead on the road God has for you and your spouse. He wants you to quiver powerlessly and hopelessly in the face of the overwhelming tide of unknowns. He wants your marriage to be overshadowed by distress and worries. He wants you to be afraid when you look at your bank account, hoping you are so distracted by fear you neglect to trust God's provision and timing. He wants you to question whether the hard work you pour into raising your children is good enough, and he wants you to try and do it all on your own strength instead of relying on the Lord. He wants stress and anxiety to consume your thoughts, so you forget to go to God in prayer. He hopes that the stress irritates you so much that you take it out on your spouse. The enemy would love nothing more than for you to be paralyzed by fear and for you to take your eyes off of God.

The only way to combat fear is to fear the only One who is worthy to be feared, God. The One who speaks things into existence from nothing. The One who holds all things together. God, our Creator and King, is the only One we should ever fear. And God, whom we fear, is also the One that loves us and "gave us a spirit not of fear but of power and love and self-control" (2 Timothy 1:7). Proverbs 9:10 tells us, "The fear of the LORD is the beginning of wisdom." Fearing God leads to life and the prolonging of it. If God is the One you fear, He will be the only One you will be interested in pleasing, and He will be the One holding all the power over your life. The fear of the enemy causes paralysis; the fear of God brings power and effectiveness. Fear God and nothing will ever shake you or stop you.

Stop right now and ask yourself, "What fears am I entertaining? What fears have kept us from pursuing God's plan for our life and marriage?"

2. LIES

You are not smart enough or qualified. What kind of impact could you make anyway? And even if you could do it, someone is already doing it better, so why waste your time? God doesn't need you; He has plenty of more effective people He is already using.

We are sure you could continue this list of phrases in your head, with all of the other "unique-to-you" lies that the enemy has whispered to your heart and mind. Let us not forget who our enemy is and what he does. Jesus himself warned us, "When [Satan] lies, he speaks out of his own character, for he is a liar and the father of lies" (John 8:44).

How can we spot the lies, especially when they seem so convincing? There is only one way to distinguish lies from truth, and it is by testing everything according to the Word of God. Replace the lies with the truth that is in God's Word and meditate on it. You must know what God says about you in His holy Word and believe it, so that when you are told something contrary, when you feel that rush of doubt or insecurity overwhelm your heart and mind, you can recognize it for what it really is, *a lie.* The enemy might try to convince you and your spouse that you are not enough, that you don't have what is required, or that you are useless to God, but with truth written on your heart, you will be able to identify and extinguish those lies quickly.

Meditate daily on the truth that is found in God's Word, letting it affirm and strengthen your heart. God says you were fearfully and wonderfully made (Psalm 139:14). You have been called by God to be holy as He is holy, therefore you can walk in holiness (1 Peter 1:14–16). You have been called out of darkness (1 Peter 2:9–10), and you have been set free (Galatians 5:1). You have been equipped by God for every good work that He has prepared for you to do (2 Timothy 3:16–17). You are strengthened by Him (Ephesians 6:10), sustained by Him (Psalm 54:4), and comforted by Him (2 Corinthians 1:3–4). Believe the truth about who you are and who your spouse is, so that when lies come to distract you from what God is doing in your life and marriage, you can boldly stand firm in faith and full of confidence of what is true.

Ask yourself right now, "What lies have I been believing about myself or my spouse? How does knowing the truth guard our effectiveness for God?"

3. SIN

Shame, brokenness, weakness, and inevitably death are the result of choosing to walk in unrepentant sin. Sinning will dismantle your effectiveness for the gospel, and it will keep you out of God's will. Our Pastor, Matt Jacobson, always tells us that "Purity is power." If you ever hope to have power in your life, you must choose to walk in purity through the power that has already been given to you through the death and resurrection of Jesus Christ.

According to the Word of God, you are no longer a slave to sin, and you have been given all things that pertain to life and godliness (2 Peter 1:3). You are no longer your own, because you have been bought for a price (1 Corinthians 7:23). Sin will have no dominion over you, since you are not under the law, but under grace (Romans 6:14). The Son has set you free, so you are free indeed (John 8:36). Believing and acting on these truths from God's Word is what sets you and your marriage apart from the rest of the world. Believing the power of Jesus Christ at work in your life, transforming your life, is the difference that others will see in you in contrast to those who do not believe. Living according to these truths helps you stand strong against the temptation to sin and empowers you to choose righteousness. Jesus, the Son of God, died for you to be set free from the power of sin and death and to reconcile you to the Father. Your purpose is sharing that incredibly good news with others.

The gospel, which means "the good news," cannot be *good* news at all if Jesus only *kind of* saved you, doing nothing to help you in your current condition. However, that is not the case! Jesus saved you completely, securing your future in heaven with the Father, and He has supplied you with power, grace, and freedom. Romans 8:11 makes it very clear, "If the Spirit of him who raised Jesus from the dead dwells in you, he who raised Christ Jesus from the dead will also give life to your mortal bodies through his Spirit who dwells in you." You are dead to sin and alive in Christ. Saturate your mind with these truths so that you will confidently believe and live out what the Spirit has already proclaimed over you.

4. SCOFFERS

When we launched Unveiledwife.com in March 2011, we had no idea what kind of response we would receive. I (Jennifer) would write an article about something we were experiencing in our marriage, and then I would share it with the handful of people who were following on social media.

After publishing only a few articles, I received a comment that was so destructive and hurtful, I immediately begged Aaron to shut the website down. This commenter didn't know us personally, and I assume she didn't consider the impact of her words, yet that didn't stop her from telling us how ungodly my husband

and I were for being open and transparent about our marriage online. We were almost derailed by her words.

This person was not the only one who didn't believe in what we were doing. Over the years we have received many nasty comments, but we thank God for His guidance and the courage He has given us to remain steadfast. We also thank God for surrounding us with faithful servants to affirm us and encourage us in our ministry. The support we received from God and other believers outweighed the impact of the scoffers, helping us to stay on track and be confident of the truth. If we had shut everything down because of the few scoffers who attacked what we were doing, we would never have heard from readers whose marriages were transformed through our ministry.

There will always be scoffers, those who are jealous, bitter, angry, skeptical, and just plain mean. The enemy uses scoffers to incite fear, doubt, and insecurity in an effort to derail faithful servants of the Lord. Scoffers will think you don't deserve your ministry, haven't earned it, aren't qualified, or believe someone else could do it better, and they share their opinions in ways that tear down instead of build up.

The solution to combating these attacks is to be confident in what God is doing in and through you, and in and through your marriage. Whether scoffers question your marriage relationship, your parenting, your business, or any ministry efforts you are pouring into, remind each other of what is true of the purpose you are pursuing together, and continue to encourage each other. Also, surround yourselves with a community of believers who will not only encourage you and walk alongside both of you as the two of you remain faithful to the specific mission God has called you to fulfill but also exhort you and hold you accountable to the truth in love. Surround yourself with Christians who will speak the life-giving words of Romans 8:31: "If God is for us, who can be against us?"

5. DIVISION

Jesus warns us, "No city or house divided against itself will stand" (Matthew 12:25). If the devil can divide you and your spouse, then he can conquer your marriage, stripping away your effectiveness for God. Why do you think there is so much divorce in our generation, even in the church? The enemy knows that he can destroy our effectiveness if he can divide our most sacred covenant, next to our relationship with God. Division almost never happens overnight; rather, it is something that starts with all of the seemingly insignificant situations and disagreements. It comes in the form of bickering and arguing, lack of communication, busyness, misplaced priorities, and unmet expectations, just to name a few. Division comes when selfishness is the motivation and pride is the platform from which the two of you interact and engage with each other.

When division ensues and a husband and wife refuse to reconcile, they are either choosing to remain forever inwardly focused, responding to each other from a place of self-preservation which leads to an unhealthy and brittle relationship, or the couple will experience the complete death of their marriage. However, the antidote to division in marriage is humility in the hearts of a husband and wife, motivating them to choose to lay aside their pride so that they may be reconciled. If they do this, they will be reunified and their effectiveness for God will remain.

Protect the unity of your marriage by walking in obedience to the Scriptures, being willing to reconcile with your spouse at any sign of discord. Adopt the perspective that you have a job to do, a mission to accomplish, a prize to win, and a treasure to build in heaven, and that this extraordinary work can only be accomplished as a team. There is strength and wisdom in numbers, and the enemy hates unity. Walk humbly in unity and use everything the Holy Spirit has given to you to fight against division.

This is not an exclusive or exhaustive list of the flaming arrows that our enemy uses to dissolve or dilute our effectiveness, but it is a start to knowing the enemy's tactics. As Christians, we must be able to recognize his tactics and then actively fight against them.

Prepare for Battle

Let's return to the story of Nehemiah for a moment. Nehemiah and his workers had a job to do—rebuild the walls of Jerusalem—but they were constantly on the verge of being attacked by their opposition. Should they stop working and fight instead? Should they run away and hide? No, because if they do either of those things, they will be doing exactly what the enemy wants, which is for the work to stop and for Nehemiah to fail. Instead, Nehemiah has the workers, all of them, strap on a sword and be ready to fight, all the while continuing to work (Nehemiah 4:17–18).

You and your spouse are spiritual people bound by the limits of physical bodies. It is very easy to forget that there is a spiritual battle raging on all around you, a real battle against real spiritual opponents. Choose to work with a sword in your hand, which is the living and active Word of God (Ephesians 6:17; Hebrews 4:12). Use this sword effectively by applying the wisdom you receive in God's Word as you pour into your marriage ministry. Defend your marriage by daily putting on the full armor that God gives you (Ephesians 6:10–18) so that you are prepared for the battle that *will* come against the ministry God has for you and your marriage. Take heart, have courage, and remember that you are not alone; you have God and the entire body of Christ on your side!

QUESTIONS FOR REFLECTION

1. In what ways have you stifled your effectiveness for God?
2. Which of the enemy's tactics—fear, lies, sin, scoffers, or division—has been employed against you? What Scripture encourages you in this battle?
3. How can you be prepared to fight the attacks of the enemy, both individually and as a couple?

Chapter 3

MARKS OF A MARRIAGE
AFTER GOD

On September 25, 2008, Jennifer uploaded a photo to her personal Facebook account. It was a picture of the two of us standing on the edge of Victoria Falls, one of the seven natural wonders of the world. We visited the spectacular waterfall during a mission trip to Africa we took shortly after we married. In the photo, we were holding each other close, smiling, and behind us a gigantic double rainbow colored the clear blue sky. We were newlyweds on an exotic adventure, but the hardships were already piling up.

From the outside looking in, and to everyone on Facebook, we had it all together. We were happy, in love, traveling the world together, and on top of all of that, we were doing it for God. What a powerful team we made. Family and friends viewing this photo would have had no idea of the pain we were actually wrestling with in our marriage. Both of us were bombarded with doubt and frustrations about our marriage, wondering why God would not help us fix the problems we were encountering. As the old adage goes, "We were faking it till we could make it."

I (Jennifer) experienced extreme pain every time Aaron and I attempted to have sex. With sex being a significant part of intimacy in marriage, I felt at fault for the frustrations we felt over this unmet expectation. Since we were not able to connect sexually, Aaron and I tried to maintain the bond of our friendship, hoping the issue would be resolved quickly. Unfortunately, there was no quick fix. The longer we went without being able to enjoy sex, the more other issues in our marriage grew. I knew Aaron struggled with pornography, and we had both assumed getting married would take away this temptation. We soon learned that this was simply not true, and in addition to this realization, our lack of sexual intimacy only worsened the problem. He wasn't loving me when he was sinning against me, and I felt I couldn't trust him. His attitude and the way he treated me changed when he kept his sin a secret. Nor was he loving God when he was sinning against Him.

I had sin in my life too, but I'll be honest—it was a lot harder for me to see. For some reason Aaron's shortcomings and sin were always easier to spot. Pride blinded me from seeing the truth of my own sin. In addition, I often told Aaron how much I missed my family and wanted to go back home. This kind of news isn't really music to a new husband's ears. He wanted me to see *him* as my family now. He understood my love for my family, but he saw through my requests to go home for what it was, discontentment with our relationship. These were some of the early hardships our marriage endured, none of which we knew how to navigate.

Our family and friends couldn't have known about our struggles because we hid them. We wanted the fairy tale,

happily-ever-after love story. We hoped God would help us figure out how to have the marriage we always wanted before it was
too late. We didn't understand at the time why God would allow
us to experience such pain and hardships in our relationship.
Instead of dealing with the issues, we stuffed our pain deep down
inside and continued to serve God together as if everything was
all right. Leading the youth at church and serving as missionaries
felt like the only things we were good at.

To say that those early years of our marriage were rough
would be an understatement. Imagine saving yourself sexually
for marriage only to find out that you and your spouse cannot
have sex! Now imagine that reality lasting for years! This was our
biggest point of marital contention, and it led to other points of
contention that eroded our oneness.

The anger that was stirred up in our hearts because we weren't
experiencing unity through sexual intimacy caused us to fight
more. We bickered too much. We had negative attitudes toward
each other, believing the lie that we were not compatible. Every
insignificant idiosyncrasy that we had amplified the problem,
adding to our discontent. The more these disconnects chipped
away at our unity, the lonelier we felt. The farther away from
each other we felt, the deeper we sank into things that could take
the pain of our brokenness away, even if just for a moment. Aaron
chose pornography, and I chose eating emotionally and escaping
through movies and books, all of it sin that took us away from
the heart of God.

Despite the effort we put into finding healing, the problem
of not being able to have sex persisted for four long years. We
were convinced we were alone in this struggle, which turned our
physical pain into emotional pain, causing us to have major spiritual

turmoil. As defeat crept into our hearts, and sin began multiplying more and more, we chose to reach out and grab for the temptations that came, severing our oneness again and again, eventually leading us to believe the lie that divorce was the only solution for us.

Although we stepped into marriage with a bold motivation to serve God together, we completely missed the mark on the kind of perspective and convictions we must have in regard to marriage in order to support the extraordinary ministry God had prepared for us to do. We deceived ourselves, convinced we could continue to praise God with our lips and tell each other we loved each other, all while our actions proved the opposite as we continued in our sin. Little did we know about the true ministry our marriage could do, if only we lived out through our actions what we believed about Christ setting us free, the very message we were preaching to others.

As we look back over those first few years of marriage, we can now see how God used our suffering to draw us closer to Him and closer to each other. We could have let anger harden our hearts and turn us away from God; we both almost got to that place, but thankfully, by the grace of God, we desperately hung onto the faith we were both raised with. Unconsciously, we both knew that saying no to our marriage would also be an ultimate no to God.

Instead, we chose to rely on God's strength each and every day, asking Him to lead us, change us, and use us. We prayed for each other and with each other. We were transparent with each other when we sinned, confessing and then reconciling with each other. We sought out Christian community, especially when we were tempted to isolate ourselves. Choosing to live out our marriage the way God wanted us to was a challenge, but the more choices we made to walk in righteousness, the more God taught us about His purpose and plan for marriage and what would be required of us in order to do His work.

What we did not realize during this time was just how far we were from understanding the importance and power of our own marriage, the importance of our ministry to *each other*. Knowing and believing God has important work for His people to do out in the world was easier to comprehend than the magnitude of work that could happen in this thing called marriage. God was in the process of showing us how a marriage that is dedicated to Him could impact the world for His glory.

We want you to know that you are not alone in your marital struggles. Your circumstances may be unique in the details, but the truth is that every marriage encounters hardship. However, we believe those hardships will play an important role in what God does in and through your marriage.

We also want you to know that just because you and your spouse have set out to serve God together, that does not guarantee a marriage free of struggles or burden. Jesus himself cautioned us, "I have said these things to you, that in me you may have peace. In the world you will have tribulation. But take heart; I have overcome the world" (John 16:33). Stand confident in the truth that in this life and in your marriage, you will encounter trials and hardship, but in Him there is peace! If you let God take charge, He will use even the most difficult trials and hardships you encounter for His glory.

Throughout our marriage, God has been pointing out specific areas of our relationship that needed to be established according to His Word. These areas are what we like to call the marks of a marriage after God. As Christians, it is our responsibility to make sure that we are living out each of these areas of marriage God's way and not our own way. We have identified seven marks of a marriage after God (see p. 238) that we believe are vital for every strong, faithful, godly couple who seeks to be effective in serving God together.

A Marriage After God Demonstrates Oneness

A marriage after God is a team moving together in one mind, one heart, one spirit, and in one direction with their eyes on heavenly and eternal things. Oneness is the joining together of a husband and wife. No longer are you two individuals experiencing life; rather, you are united as one flesh (Genesis 2:24). One flesh does not mean two independent individuals sometimes acting as one, neither does it mean two individuals negotiating a workable schedule where they inhabit the same space but leave each other alone. One flesh is a picture of unity, a joining together, a growing together, where parts of each other are woven together in a way that there is no noticeable seam.

Oneness is one of the greatest ways we show the world the true gospel. Before He died, Jesus prayed that His followers would be unified: "I in them and you in me, that they may become perfectly one, so that the world may know that you sent me and loved them even as you loved me" (John 17:23).

Paul brings more color to this concept of oneness when he writes, "In the same way husbands should love their wives as their own bodies. He who loves his wife loves himself" (Ephesians 5:28). What a powerful argument! Paul points out that there is no closer relationship one could have than to oneself, and that is exactly how we are supposed to see our spouse, as ourselves.

ONENESS is one of the **GREATEST** ways we show the world the **TRUE** gospel.

Oneness, not two-ness. Not me and her-ness or me and him-ness. Oneness. You and your spouse have been united as one. Determining in your heart and mind that you are one is crucial, for from this you will draw the way you respond to each other and to the world. It doesn't matter if you have separate jobs. It doesn't matter if you have separate passions, desires, or talents. You are one flesh. Over time the oneness of your unity, the bond that weaves you into one with no noticeable seam, will get stronger and stronger. How do you do this practically? Let the beautiful words of Philippians 2:1–4 guide you: "So if there is any encouragement in Christ, any comfort from love, any participation in the Spirit, any affection and sympathy, complete my joy by being of the same mind, having the same love, being in full accord and of one mind. Do nothing from selfish ambition or conceit, but in humility count others more significant than yourselves. Let each of you look not only to his own interests, but also to the interests of others."

A marriage after God is a single unit, moving in the same direction, convictions held to the same doctrine, and motivated by the same vision. Your pursuits and priorities in life should never be motivated by selfish ambition, nor should you put your own interests above your spouse. We understand that your current marriage relationship may not live up to this ideal; to be honest, our own marriage often falls short as well. Marriage is a journey of sanctification and transformation for the purpose of bringing God glory, and the journey is always ongoing. What we have found along the way is that once you embrace the reality that you are no longer two separate individuals like you were when you were single, but that you and your spouse are one, you will begin to see that the two of you are stronger together.

If you are not one with each other, your marriage will be vulnerable to destruction. Mark 3:24 says, "If a kingdom is divided against itself, that kingdom cannot stand." Either you are one with your spouse or are a broken-down kingdom, and a broken-down kingdom cannot expand its kingdom because it is either in shambles or is striving to build up its own foundation and walls again. Protect your marriage by choosing to embrace the power of unity by being one with your spouse.

A Marriage After God Demonstrates Submission

A marriage after God is completely submitted to the Lord in action, will, desires, finances, parenting, and every other part of life. A marriage after God understands derived authority and lives according to the order God has placed in regard to our most intimate relationship.

Let us use Paul's instruction to wives to illustrate this concept, as God intended: "Wives, submit to your own husbands, as to the Lord. For the husband is the head of the wife even as Christ is the head of the church, his body, and is himself its Savior. Now as the church submits to Christ, so also wives should submit in everything to their husbands" (Ephesians 5:22–24). Not only is this a clear instruction on how a wife is to operate in her marriage, but it is also a divine mystery, showing how the church is to operate in its relationship with Christ. We are the church, the bride of Christ, His people. We are to submit in everything to Him and His leadership, just as the wife is to submit to her husband.

Is God on the throne in your marriage? When you make decisions are they submitted first to Him with a humble and yielded heart? What about sin? Submission isn't required only in the big decisions of life but also in our holiness. As believers, we are no longer slaves to sin and have been given the beautiful opportunity to become slaves of righteousness. Romans 6:13 declares, "Do not present your members to sin as instruments for unrighteousness, but present yourselves to God as those who have been brought from death to life, and your members to God as instruments for righteousness."

Submission to God and submission to His holy Word is the only position that a believer can take, for we are God's people and we have been created to fulfill His purposes. It is not about us; rather, it is about the Lord and what He desires. As you submit to God in your personal relationship with Him, you will reap the rich fruit that will be produced through your obedience, the evidence of which will be seen in and through your marriage.

A Marriage After God Is Biblical

A marriage after God is one that declares, "All that the LORD has spoken we will do" (Exodus 19:8). A marriage after God is not only interested in serving God through extraordinary work; a marriage after God is interested in living out a biblical marriage.

As we strongly stated in chapter 1, the Bible is our foundation and our point of reference for how to conduct ourselves. For example, when Scripture tells us to love one another (John 13:34), be at peace with one another (Mark 9:50), serve one another (Galatians 5:13), and forgive one another (Ephesians 4:32), these are principles we are commanded to live out every day toward everyone, especially the closest "one another" in our life, our spouse. As biblical people, we strive to walk in the

Spirit (Galatians 5:16) so that our spouse and others can taste the goodness of the Lord through the fruit being produced in our lives. We conduct ourselves in a worthy manner, full of love, joy, peace, patience, kindness, goodness, faithfulness, gentleness, and self-control (Galatians 5:22–23). Not because we just decided those were great virtues to have, but because God's Word has directed us in such a way, and His Spirit empowers us to do so.

John 1 tells us that Jesus is the Word. If we claim to follow Jesus, then we must read the Word, know the Word, and follow the Word. We must know Jesus and we must choose to follow Him and the example He set for us. Be fully submitted to the culture and authority of the Word. Choose to be biblical people who listen to the Lord's instruction through the teaching in His Word. Be doers of the Word.

A marriage after God is one that keeps God at the center of their relationship and follows His guidance, using the truth of His Word. Their hearts and minds are aligned with the Lord's and they walk humbly with each other, living together in an understanding way.

A Marriage After God Is Sacrificial

A marriage after God is one where the husband and wife have recognized that their spiritual maturity is infinitely more important than momentary comfort and personal gratification. Therefore, a marriage after God inevitably involves sacrifice. Paul says, "I appeal to you therefore, brothers, by the mercies of God, to present your bodies as a living sacrifice, holy and acceptable to God, which is your spiritual worship" (Romans 12:1). The difference between a dead sacrifice and a living sacrifice is that a dead sacrifice can't decide to move once placed on the altar, whereas a living sacrifice can choose to get up and crawl away. As living sacrifices, choose to stay right where God wants you, with your lives laid down before Him.

As you and your spouse live out your days as a living sacrifice to God, there will be moments when God will ask the two of you to give up things you may enjoy or things that provide you comfort. He may ask you to lay down your hobbies, your jobs, your time, your energy, your money, your plans, or your dreams. There are many reasons why God might ask you to lay these things down, perhaps to teach you something new, mature you, reveal an important perspective to you, prepare the way for something new, or all of the above. No matter what God asks you to give up, whether it is for a season or for good, you know you can confidently trust Him and trust His will for you and your marriage.

Consider the story of Jesus and the rich young man. All his life this young man had obeyed God's commands, but Jesus saw into his heart and told him, "You lack one thing: go, sell all that you have and give to the poor, and you will have treasure in heaven; and come, follow me" (Mark 10:21). Sadly, the man walked away disheartened because he had great wealth and did not want to sacrifice it to follow Jesus. In that moment the man was given a choice between Jesus and his wealth. The choice was his, and he chose to walk away.

As a husband and wife, you will have to sacrifice things such as your pride, perhaps your finances, or your time. A marriage after God says yes to God, even when our flesh screams no!

Choose to be a living sacrifice by offering your whole life to God. Give God access to every part of your life and marriage, and if there are things that He asks you to give up or let go of, yield your heart to Him.

A marriage after God says **YES** to God, even when our flesh screams **NO!**

A Marriage After God Is Transparent

A marriage after God is one where the husband and wife are transparent with one another. Transparency in marriage is like giving your spouse a flashlight and letting them explore the depths of your heart. Transparency is being honest with your spouse through the art of communication, talking to one another, sharing details of your circumstances, emotions, past, sins, and anything else that the Holy Spirit moves you to share. This is how a husband and wife truly get to know each other. It may feel risky and your flesh will be tempted to avoid this, but if you want to experience extraordinary intimacy with your spouse, be vulnerable with them. Let light cast off any shadows that may be lurking deep inside. Being a husband and wife who walk in light with one another, refusing to walk in darkness, is how you and your spouse practice truth and experience fellowship with one another. Let 1 John 1:5–7 encourage you and guide you in this practice: "This is the message we have heard from him and proclaim to you, that God is light, and in him is no darkness at all. If we say we have fellowship with him while we walk in darkness, we lie and do not practice the truth. But if we walk in the light, as he is in the light, we have fellowship with one another, and the blood of Jesus his Son cleanses us from all sin."

A husband and wife after God are not only transparent with one another, but they are also a couple who actively engages with and are transparent with fellow Christians. Proverbs 18:1 warns us, "Whoever isolates himself seeks his own desire; he breaks out against all sound judgment." People can be quick to justify why they don't need to be a part of the body of Christ, or they convince themselves they are walking in community, yet they refuse to be transparent with those they are walking with. Unfortunately, those who do not participate in Christian fellowship do not have the benefit of the body being near to encourage them through tough times, support them, serve them, or sharpen them. Isolation is disobedience and will hinder the ministry God has for you. Transparency is rare in relationships today, but you don't have to miss out on the benefit it provides in deepening your relationships. Be someone who chooses transparency.

A Marriage After God Is Intimate

A marriage after God relentlessly pursues and embraces intimacy with each other and with God.

Our greatest example of this level of intimacy is, of course, Jesus. He put His hands on people who no one else would dare to touch (Luke 5:13); He reached down and held a dying little girl's hand, giving her life again (Mark 5:41); He broke cultural taboos to talk to people (John 4:9); and He wept over the death of His close friend (John 11:35). That's our Savior. He embraced intimacy. If we are not intimate with God, we cannot be intimate with other people. We cannot weep with those who weep or mourn with those who mourn or laugh with those who laugh. We must look to the example of Christ and be willing to embrace intimacy, with God and in our marriage.

You can know God intimately by becoming familiar with His Word, communicating to Him through prayer, worshiping Him through obedience, and praising Him with songs. Intimacy in your relationship with God will only be cultivated as you do these things out of your deep love for Him. Consistently spending time with God will create the atmosphere for intimacy to thrive. Embrace intimacy with God by getting to know Him and take time to share your heart with Him.

Marital intimacy also requires spending quality time together and sharing your hearts with one another. Intimacy will never happen if the only way you connect or communicate is through text messages or rushed conversations. It wouldn't take very long for problems to arise in a marriage like that, or for a feeling of rejection to creep in.

Intimacy in marriage will require you to initiate. A husband and wife have emotional and physical needs that can be filled through affection, communication, date nights, and daily prayer. Protect the intimacy in your relationship with your spouse by fighting for it instead of fighting against it. Fight against fear, pride, or anything else that might get in the way of experiencing the binding and unifying power of intimacy between you and your spouse. Share your hearts by telling each other how you are feeling, what you are thinking, or what you are learning. Be willing to touch each other and make one another feel loved. Be willing to get to know your spouse by studying them. Get to know their likes and dislikes. If you are familiar with these things, you will know when and how to affirm your spouse, which creates a safe place for intimacy to develop.

A Marriage After God Is a Good Example to Others

A marriage after God is one that others can imitate. Paul gives the Corinthian church this charge, "Be imitators of me, as I am of Christ" (1 Corinthians 11:1). Can you and your spouse confidently invite another couple to follow your example? Can you encourage your children to follow your example? If your answer to these questions is no, we urge you to implement the truth of God's Word in your marriage, to choose to walk in righteousness, and to be the positive example this world desperately needs. Take a look at the world, so lacking in love, respect, and peace. There is a desperate need for examples of mature individuals and relationships. We need couples who can show what it looks like to have an extraordinary marriage, a marriage centered on God.

Examples of godly marriages help others see how they can get to where they want to be. Examples of God-fearing married couples encourage others to persevere in hard times. Examples of marriages after God inspire others and show them how to faithfully build the kingdom of God. Can you imagine what our world would look like if we had these examples?

So how do you become a godly example to the world, to your neighbor, to your children? You practice righteousness, consistently choosing to obey God and love others (1 John 3:4–10). The choice is yours. Are you choosing to do what God has called you to do? Are you faithful and steadfast in your relationship with God and with each other? Are you a person of integrity, choosing righteousness even when no one is around or looking at you as an example? Every choice you make, whether big or small, has the potential to make you an example worth following or not.

If you are never in the Word, how can you encourage others to be? If you don't have self-control or if you don't pray, how can you encourage others to do those things?

The example you are setting for the world can be incredibly powerful. But even more important is the example you set for your spouse and children. You have an obligation to your family to live in a way that will reflect the example of Christ in your home. Just as Paul sets his aim on imitating Christ, make it a priority to imitate Christ so that your family, and then the world, can see God through you. With Christ as your model, may you and your marriage set an example others can follow.

Watch for the Rainbow

The rainbow at Victoria Falls was vibrant that day, so close it seemed as though we could reach out and touch it. Looking at our photo now and remembering how God sent a rainbow to Noah as a sign of His faithfulness (Genesis 9:12–17), I (Aaron) am reminded that God's promises never fail, even when we fail. I am reminded that He is with us always, even when hardships seem to surround us. Because we submitted to the Lord and obeyed Him, He was able to use the trials and suffering my wife and I faced to teach us who He is and the purpose He has for marriage. The marks of a marriage after God were not always easy things for us to understand and implement, but by practicing them we began to comprehend them. God took two broken and wretched people, teetering on the edge of separation, and transformed us into a whole and healthy couple whose marriage is built on a secure foundation. And now, after years of intentionally pursuing God's desire for our marriage, we are beginning to see the fruit that comes from abiding in Him and obeying His Word.

You are in the midst of pursuing God's desire for your marriage. That is one of the reasons you are reading this book! You might be at the beginning of the journey or you may be far down the road, or maybe you are somewhere in the middle. No matter where you are, God desires the same for every marriage: to walk in obedience to His Word.

Every marriage will encounter various obstacles along the way. What sets a marriage after God apart is that the husband and wife trust in God as they learn to minister to each other. God is with you and your spouse. He is faithful, and He is trustworthy, as Paul reminds us: "If we are faithless, he remains faithful" (2 Timothy 2:13).

Please remember that in the midst of hardships, and while God is transforming your hearts, you will have opportunities to stand side by side with your spouse and marvel at the wonderful works of God. Recognizing those moments will draw your hearts close to His and give you hope for the future. Yes, at times you may feel that the rain is pouring down and will never stop, but in those times keep your focus on the Word of God. Be reminded of His promises for you and all that He desires for you. Submit your heart to God and choose to walk in obedience to His Word and encourage your spouse to do the same. Do this, and the marks of a marriage after God will be true and evident in your life.

QUESTIONS FOR REFLECTION

1. Review the seven marks of a marriage after God. Which mark is most difficult for you to implement? Which mark is most motivating to you?
2. Reflect on your relationship. Have there been "rainbow moments" when God showed His faithfulness to you as a couple? How does that memory comfort and inspire you?

Part 2

BUILDING A STRONG FOUNDATION:
THE PREPARATION

Chapter 4

YOUR RELATIONSHIP
WITH THE BIBLE

Jennifer and I purchased our first home in 2016, just after celebrating our ninth anniversary. However, although our names were on the title and the keys were in our hands confirming that we were the owners, we didn't get to move in immediately because the house was in need of a complete remodel.

Our house was built in 1965 and hadn't been lived in for over three years. The wiring in the attic resembled a rat's nest. The ceilings sagged, and the guest bathroom lacked both a vanity and plumbing. The previous owner had done a lot of work on the house, but these "upgrades" were not completed to code and needed to be fully removed and replaced. With the help of Cody, a good friend of ours, we began to transform the broken-down house into a beautiful home for our growing family.

The process of remodeling our home took a little over three months to finish. Besides the repairs, we also decided to add about 170 square feet to our main living room. We hired a local company to frame the foundation of the addition and pour the concrete. When I went to the house to check the concrete, however, I noticed a disturbing problem. What was supposed to be our solid new foundation instead had sections that were cracked, crumbling, and even falling off. This foundation not only needed to bear the weight of the walls but also the new roof line and trusses for the entire length of the living room. Needless to say, I was worried.

I quickly called up Cody and explained the problem. After coming over and evaluating the situation, he advised me to rip out the entire foundation and repour the concrete to make sure the foundation would be sound. This added extra time and money to an already enormous overhaul, but correcting the foundation was absolutely necessary. Otherwise, that part of our home would be unstable and unreliable.

Although the work would delay our move-in date by two weeks, we chose to start over. The new concrete was poured and set perfectly. The walls went up, and we knew we had made the right decision. As soon as the renovations were complete, we moved in and began to unpack. Now we have confidence in the house we built. Our home is sturdy, stable, and reliable, and it serves its purpose for our family. We use our living room every day, multiple times a day . . . and you know what? We don't ever think about the concrete foundation holding us up. We don't need to think about it, because we know it is secure and strong.

Just as a house needs a strong foundation to stand the test of time, a marriage after God also must have a strong and firm foundation. If you have been married for some time, there may be parts of your relationship that need remodeling. There may be parts that are fractured, unable to withstand the weight of the work that God has for your marriage. Or perhaps you and your spouse are just getting started on building the foundation. No matter where you are on the journey, we want you to be able to stand firm as you and your spouse boldly chase after God's vision and call for your marriage.

We want you, too, to experience the benefit and blessing of having a strong foundation for your marriage. If the foundation is weak, the building will not stand for long. If the foundation is not level, the building will lean and eventually fall. You must consider the importance of having a strong and level marriage foundation, for from it you will build your marriage, your family, and the ministry work God has prepared for you to do.

So what is the firm foundation on which to build your marriage? It is, of course, the Word of God. In chapter 1, we introduced the fact that you must decide what you believe about the Word of God. The Bible can be only one of two things: either it is the inspired, inerrant, complete, and living Word of God; or it is nothing.

In our pursuit of an extraordinary marriage, we had to decide whether or not we were going to believe the Bible to be what it says it is. We ultimately decided to yield our hearts to the truth of the Bible, and as a result we have seen God move in our life and marriage in ways we could never have dreamed or imagined. God has used His Word to continually grow us and mature us into the people He created us to be.

Because you are reading this book, we know you also desire to grow closer to God and to each other. So take a moment to examine the foundation of your marriage. Look at your life to see whether it exhibits the following four habits. First, do you read the Bible daily? Second, do you listen to the Bible? Third, do you meditate on the Bible? And finally, do you obey the Bible? These four habits will establish God's Word as the firm foundation on which to build your marriage and your ministry. Let's take a moment to look at them more closely.

Do You Read the Bible Daily?

According to the 2018 Barna Group survey on the state of Bible reading in our country, only 14 percent of people surveyed say they read the Bible daily. Fourteen percent? Meanwhile, 13 percent read it several times a week, 8 percent use it once a week, 6 percent consult it monthly, and 8 percent open the Bible a few times a year. That leaves 51 percent of the people surveyed who say they *never* read the Bible.[1] These are not good numbers, especially for people who claim to base their entire faith on the book that they aren't even reading.

Where do you fall in these numbers? Is reading Scripture a daily habit in your home? Do you open the Word of God daily and even multiple times a day? Is the Bible a defining factor in your marriage? If you have children, do you engage in daily family Bible time with them?

Admittedly, even as I (Aaron) am writing this, I am being convicted about our relationship with this divine book. If we truly believe that the Bible is the inspired Word of God (2 Timothy 3:16), then we should have a strong desire to open it up and read it. How can we say we believe one way and act another? Thanks be to

---

1 Barna, "State of the Bible 2018: Seven Top Findings," July 10, 2018, https://www.barna.com/research/state-of-the-bible-2018-seven-top-findings/.

God that He is patient and kind and does not base our salvation on how much we read His Word. But let us not use this as an excuse for why we do not open and read this love letter from our Creator.

Don't let your heart drift away from the solid, unchanging, ever relevant, and ever transformative Word of God. Ignite in your heart the passion and drive for the life-giving words found between the covers of the Holy Bible. Become like the "noble" Bereans, who "received the word with all eagerness, examining the Scriptures daily to see if these things were so" (Acts 17:11).

Do You Listen to the Bible?

The practice of listening to the Word of God is as old as time itself. Adam and Eve could only listen to what God would say to them, for nothing had been written yet. Abraham heard God speak; the people of Israel heard God through the voices of the prophets; and now we hear the Word of God taught by those with the gift of teaching. We need to come together regularly with other believers to hear God's Word and encourage each other (Hebrews 10:25). Listening to the Word of God read aloud by others and listening to teaching from the Word of God are indispensable for our biblical understanding, retention, and most importantly the bolstering of our Christian faith. Paul himself teaches that "faith comes from hearing, and hearing through the word of Christ" (Romans 10:17).

Walk in the example of the early Christians, who "devoted themselves to the apostles' teaching and the fellowship, to the breaking of bread and the prayers" (Acts 2:42). Be steadfast in the hearing of the Word and encourage your spouse to hear the Word, so that the foundation of your faith may stand firm.

Do You Meditate on the Bible?

Biblical meditation is very different from how the world might define meditation, for it is very active, in contrast to worldly meditation, which teaches a passive experience of emptying or clearing the mind. Meditating on the Word consists of filling yourself with Scripture, actively speaking it, memorizing it, and delighting in it, then repeating this process over and over again throughout your days.

Biblical meditation is like a cow chewing its cud. When a cow grazes in a field, it pulls up nutrient-rich grass, which is dense and tough, chews a bit, then swallows it until she is full. She will then bring back up the chewed grass, which is called cud, and will continue to chew on it some more. This process is how cows break down and glean all the nutrients they can from the grass. Now, consider how this can be translated to meditating on the Word of God. You read the Word, you chew on it and draw from its nutrients, so that while you are not reading it, you can then speak the words you read to yourself and to your spouse throughout the day, recalling those Scriptures moment by moment, being nourished by it. Make Psalm 119:15–16 your daily pursuit: "I will meditate on your precepts and fix my eyes on your ways. I will delight in your statutes; I will not forget your word."

Do You Obey the Bible?

All this reading, meditating, and memorizing the Word of God means absolutely nothing if it does not equate to a change in your life and behavior. James strongly warns us to not just be hearers

All this reading, meditating, and memorizing the Word of God means absolutely **NOTHING** if it does not equate to a change in your life and behavior.

of the Word, but doers of the Word (James 1:22). Christians who read the Word but do not allow it to transform them contribute to the world's belief that Christians are hypocrites. A marriage after God is one that is eager to allow the Word of God to transform them by the power of the Holy Spirit. This part of your foundation is what will make your marriage effective for the kingdom of God. If God's Word says to take up your cross and follow Him, or pray without ceasing, or submit, or love, *do you?*

The Word was given to us to change us. Yes, God loved us so much that while we were still sinners He sent His Son to die for us (Romans 5:8), but, as someone once said, "He loves us too much to leave us that way." Your heavenly Father, like any good father, desires that you and your spouse would mature and become the man and woman that He has called you to be. His Word is the seed that He intends to grow in you to produce good fruit. As Paul wrote, "But as for you, continue in what you have learned and have firmly believed, knowing from whom you learned it and how from childhood you have been acquainted with the sacred writings, which are able to make you wise for salvation through faith in Christ Jesus. All Scripture is breathed out by God and profitable for teaching, for reproof, for correction, and for training in righteousness, that the man of God may be complete, equipped for every good work" (2 Timothy 3:14–17).

You already know how vital the Bible is to the Christian life, especially a marriage after God. Keep pressing onward, using the Bible to guide you as you build or rebuild your marriage foundation. Emphasize it, highlight it, elevate it to its proper place in your world. Prioritize it and practice what it says. Allow the Word of God to shape your thoughts and desires. Allow it to permeate your heart in such a way that others, including your spouse, recognize the supremacy of the Bible in your life, and are driven by curiosity to ask why you stand so firmly upon it. You can trust this: commitment to this practice will never be wasted.

As the next three chapters will show, the Bible stands as a firm foundation for the building of a strong marriage, a strong community, and a strong financial framework. Make the foundation strong and the building will be strong. Make the foundation weak and the building will not stand. Build on the Word of God and you will have confidence in the building, just like we have confidence in the addition to our home, having no doubt that it will accomplish what it was built for.

QUESTIONS FOR REFLECTION

1. Which habit do you most need to incorporate into your life? How will you do that?
2. How can you encourage each other to develop good habits when it comes to reading, listening to, meditating on, and obeying Scripture?

Chapter 5

YOUR FIRST MINISTRY

My wife and I welcomed our first son into the world at the tail end of 2012. That next year we experienced a handful of challenging transitions that dramatically impacted our life and marriage. The first transition was learning how to be good parents. This new experience was a steep learning curve for both of us, yet we embraced it with earnestness, knowing children are a blessing from God.

During this same season my wife and I self-published *Wife After God*. Not only that, we navigated changes in my job, including a change in my position and a location move that cost me two hours of traffic each way, every day. We also began to consider two significant opportunities, including publishing our marriage story and a move out of state. It was a busy year for us, motivating us to pray even more, trusting in God that He would guide us through.

When our son was a year and a half, we moved forward on both of these opportunities. We began the process of writing our first traditionally published book, *The Unveiled Wife*, and we moved to a beautiful town in Central Oregon. Although we were new in town, we had a few relationships to help pave the way. One of those relationships was with our literary agent, Matt, who would later become our mentor and pastor. Within a few weeks of our move, we went to lunch with Matt, assuming it would be a time to get to know each other better and talk about the book business. Little did we know that "getting to know each other" would go deeper than we ever expected.

We met up with Matt at a local place called Spork, a popular fusion food joint, known for its creative spin on dishes from Latin America, Asia, and Africa. We ordered our food, found a table next to the window, and started chatting. We caught him up on the move, the progress of writing the book, and how our son was handling it all. Everything we shared was at surface level, until Matt asked me (Aaron) one very pointed question. Looking right into my eyes, he asked, "Does your wife feel cherished by you?"

I sank a little in my chair, contemplating the weight of this question.

He followed up with a second question: "Can your wife honestly say that she is the most cherished woman in the world?"

I sank deeper. My wife sat next to me, making the question even harder to answer.

As I glanced over at Jennifer, I could tell she felt just as unprepared and uncomfortable as I did. The truth was that I had no idea how to answer Matt's question. For a moment, I was speechless. I decided to direct the question to my wife and let her answer for me, which made this experience all the more awkward, because she didn't know how to answer the question either. She smiled with embarrassment and distracted the attention away from herself by tending to our son. Our responses revealed the answer. Neither one of us could confidently say yes.

This knowledge broke my heart.

With only a few words, I had been confronted with the hypocrisy of our ministry. We had been participating in and leading "marriage ministry" for a few years now. We had blogs and social media platforms with thousands of couples gleaning marriage encouragement from us daily. We had books that helped readers grow closer to God and their spouse. Despite these signs of our success and leadership, none of these things meant anything to the man sitting across the table from us, who had deep concern and love in his heart for the true condition of our marriage.

In this moment our agent, being a godly and wise man, knew that if any of our "ministry" was to be long-lasting and effective, it needed to first be true in our own marriage. He wasn't insinuating that our marriage was bad or broken. He wasn't assuming that we were unqualified or unprepared for what we were doing. However, he was simply saying to us with this bold question that none of our ministry outside of our marriage matters if our marriage isn't recognized and prioritized in our hearts as our first ministry.

There would be no pursuit, purpose, or ministry opportunity great enough to chase after if we did not see each other as the first and most important people we were called to minister to.

I finally cut the miserably embarrassing silence with an honest evaluation of my relationship with my wife. "I don't know if she could say that." As the words came out of my mouth, my wife confirmed this reality with a slight shake of her head. We loved each other; that much we both knew. At this point in our marriage we knew we would persevere together come what may. Also, we were happily serving God in ways that confirmed in our hearts that God created us and joined us together for a great purpose. Yet, in the day-to-day planning and executing of the goals we had established, we still sometimes neglected our marriage. There was a gap in our intimacy, one that if left unchecked had the potential to erode our relationship and also our ministry. My wife needed to know and be confident that I cherished her, and it broke my heart to realize that I wasn't doing that.

Our new friend wasn't done yet.

Next Matt turned to Jennifer and asked, "Would your husband agree that he is the most respected man in the world?"

There was another uncomfortable silence. Then Matt said, "You don't need to answer these questions right now, but I want you two to consider the importance of fulfilling what God has called you to fulfill in your relationship with each other."

He then cautioned us that if we did not believe that our marriage was the first ministry God has entrusted to us, if we did not pour into each other the way God desires us and commands us to, than we would be in grave and certain danger of losing what God had given to us . . . not just our ministries, but more sadly, our marriage. He warned us that just as quickly as God had given it all to us, it could all, just as quickly, be lost.

Probing Questions

This confrontation stirred up some probing questions as I considered my failure to cherish my wife. How much was I actually pursuing her heart? How often did I consider her emotional and spiritual desires and needs? Was my affection toward her obvious, or present at all? As difficult as it was to admit to another man in front of my wife that I was not fulfilling my responsibility in my marriage, it forced me to evaluate what God desired of my wife and me and the necessity of being obedient to His Word.

Am I the man that I am encouraging other men to be? Am I a biblical husband, actively loving my wife by meeting her needs, living with her in an understanding way, washing her by the Word?

Is my wife the woman she is encouraging other wives to be? Is she a biblical wife, showing respect for me and my leadership? Does she have a heart of submission? Does she have a gentle and quiet spirit?

Does our marriage proclaim the good news of the gospel to this world by demonstrating sacrificial love, grace, and unity?

In Ephesians 5 God clearly conveys that love and respect are required in marriage. As a husband, I am called to cherish and love my wife just as Christ does the church. My wife is called to respect me and submit to me as the church does to Christ. We knew these Scriptures well, yet we were not adequately fulfilling them. We had started our marriage with the best of intentions, but as we encountered hardship, our love and respect for each other eroded. We loved each other, of course. That was an easy thing to say, but our actions didn't always match up. We still bickered over meaningless things, we each prioritized our own pleasures, and we both wrestled with pride.

The message we got that afternoon was serious. I realized that we were more motivated to grow our "marriage ministry" than we were to grow our own relationship. At that time we were not enduring hardships, but we definitely were not putting each other first. We both were exhausting ourselves every day creating and maintaining content to encourage other marriages, while only sporadically nurturing ours. Our priorities were out of order.

Through Matt, God was challenging us to mature, to be transformed, to live out the very message we were encouraging others to live out, to be the husband and wife, and the parents,

God intended us to be. We had to stop being fulfilled by the ministry we were doing, even though we were doing it together, and spend some intentional time prioritizing our marriage and family. We had to learn how to keep and maintain this order if we were going to continue in any ministry work the Lord had for us to do. We had to recognize the truth that the ministry we were called to do was first toward each other.

We want you and your spouse to consider the same mind-shifting questions we received that day. Intentionally cherishing and respecting each other are vital parts of your marriage ministry. As you consider your own marriage, ask yourself honestly: Are there gaps in our relationship? Are we currently pursuing any ministry work or prioritizing any other endeavor or relationship above our marriage and family? If your answer to these questions is yes, we challenge you to readjust and consider the truth that your marriage is your first ministry, and when you faithfully pursue this ministry, it will pour over into every other ministry God has for you.

Be Faithful

The news of a Christian couple ending their relationship in divorce has become heartbreakingly too familiar to us. Unfortunately, because of its frequency and regularity, the shock that we should be feeling from this kind of news is almost all but lost. The reality is that divorce and scandal happen often in Christian marriages, including even those who consider themselves in "ministry." Has it always been this way? Are marriages simply too hard to maintain? Or have Christians lost their perspective of the purpose and priority of marriage?

Sadly, there have been too many Christians who do ministry

in the name of serving God yet neglect their first ministry to their spouse. With incremental choices, they work too long and too hard, they neglect their spouse, they seek sexual or emotional intimacy outside of marriage, and they live as hypocrites. In their disobedience to God they give room to their flesh and to the enemy to bring destruction not just to their marriages and the ministry work they do but also to the name of God in this world.

As long as Christian husbands and wives see ministry to be separate from everything else in life instead of ministry being their life, they will never be able to recognize the true value of their marriage.

We must never sacrifice our marriages on the altar of "ministry." We cannot put off our duty as a husband and wife for the duties of the "church." If Christian believers are the ones who make up the church, and a husband and wife are believers, do they not have an obligation to treat one another as the body of Christ? If we are believers, then we are the church, and our marriages are our first and foremost ministry.

How do we know this is true? How can we be sure that God is pleased when His people turn their hearts toward their spouse and toward their children? All we have to do is search His Word. In the final pages of the Old Testament, in the book of Malachi, God rebukes the people of Judah for their broken marriages and families:

> You cover the LORD's altar with tears, with weeping and groaning because he no longer regards the offering or accepts it with favor from your hand. But you say, "Why does he not?" Because the LORD was witness between you and the wife of your youth, to whom you have been faithless, though she is

your companion and your wife by covenant. Did he not make them one, with a portion of the Spirit in their union? And what was the one God seeking? Godly offspring. So guard yourselves in your spirit, and let none of you be faithless to the wife of your youth. "For the man who does not love his wife but divorces her, says the LORD, the God of Israel, covers his garment with violence, says the LORD of hosts. So guard yourselves in your spirit, and do not be faithless" (Malachi 2:13–16).

God tells His people that He has witnessed their unfaithfulness to their wives, which hindered their ability to raise children who knew and loved Him. Our marriages and families are important to God. Marriage was created and established by God, the symbol He chose to reveal His message of love to the world. Let us not make the same mistake the people of Judah did. Let us not fall to the temptations that try to draw our hearts away from marriage and family. Let us not be Christians who misrepresent the gospel of God's unconditional love and amazing grace by walking in sin. Let us not be faithless.

Rather, let us be men and women who treat their marriage as their first ministry—always. Let us choose to walk in faithfulness.

As we learned in chapter 1, Adam and Eve's job was to be fruitful and multiply and subdue the earth. If Adam had left Eve to pursue God's ministry alone, he would have failed. Adam could not have been fruitful and multiplied without his bride. Likewise, Eve could not have been Adam's helper in the job of subduing the earth if she went off to do it her way without him. Adam and Eve were united as one, and their ministry had to be accomplished together in order for God's purposes to be fulfilled.

The ministry God has for your marriage is no different than

Our MARRIAGES and FAMILIES are IMPORTANT to God.

what He commanded those first two humans. Here is what the order of ministry focus looks like in a healthy, biblical marriage:

1. You and your spouse's relationship with God
2. Your marriage relationship
3. You and your spouse's relationship with your children
4. Then everything else

If any of these relationships are out of order, the fruit of your ministry will be hindered. Maybe it will not be evident immediately, but your lack of faithfulness to maintain this order will eventually reveal itself for what it is.

To make your marriage your first ministry, you must see you and your spouse as a single body. Remember Paul's exhortation: "In the same way husbands should love their wives as their own bodies. He who loves his wife loves himself. For no one ever hated his own flesh, but nourishes and cherishes it, just as Christ does the church, because we are members of his body" (Ephesians 5:28–30).

If we recognize our spouse as one with us, we will take care of them the way we take care of ourselves, nourishing, cherishing, and loving our spouse as much as we do ourselves, just like Christ does for His own body, the church. When you operate as one in your marriage, you are not only fulfilling a command of the Lord, but you are also walking in a way that trains you and prepares you for ministry outside the home. Not viewing your marriage in this way does the exact opposite, by emaciating your body and making it less capable of actualizing God's mission for you and your marriage. Just like an athlete trains, feeds, and prepares their body to win a race, you are called to nourish your "body," preparing and training your marriage for the race set before you.

Take a moment and honestly evaluate the way you treat your spouse to see if you are nourishing or neglecting your marriage spiritually, mentally, emotionally, or physically. Are you and your spouse walking in the unity of one heart, one mind, and one spirit? Or are you divided? If you are divided or struggling, that means you are weak, and if you are weak, then you will be unprepared and ineffective for any ministry work God has prepared for your life.

Ministering well in marriage and in parenting means choosing to walk faithfully in the greatest commandment the Lord ever gave: "You shall love the Lord your God with all your heart and with all your soul and with all your mind. This is the great and first commandment. And a second is like it: You shall love your neighbor as yourself" (Matthew 22:37–39). Love God and love your neighbor—that's it! And as we always say when talking with couples: Your closest neighbor is your spouse!

Marriage is your first ministry because you and your spouse have the opportunity to minister to each other every day as you love each other with the love of God. Your marriage is also your first ministry because as you two lavish each other with God's divine love, you reflect the love between Christ and His bride to others. Choosing to love in the easy times and in the more difficult seasons of marriage will have a profound impact in your spouse's life, in your children's lives, and in the lives of others as they witness and experience God's love pouring out of you. Choosing to love is much more powerful and a necessity in marriage, in contrast to the "falling" in and out of love that the world portrays as the way of life. God desires us to choose unconditional love, just like He chose to love us when He sent His Son to be a sacrifice for our sake.

We are patient and kind to our spouse because God is patient and kind with us. We are not arrogant or rude, but rather, we are humble and gentle with our spouse, because that is how God is toward us. We are faithful to our spouse because God is faithful to us. We are loving to our spouse because God is loving toward us. We forgive because He first forgave us.

One of the greatest benefits of your marriage being your first ministry is that it is where you practice your ministry to the rest of the world. Your marriage is the message you are preaching to others. The way you and your spouse interact with each other reveals the gospel you believe.

If your spouse doesn't experience the gospel in your marriage, how could you ever hope to share the gospel with anyone else? If your spouse never practices reconciliation with you, how could they ever teach someone about the reconciling nature of God? If the two of you do not love each other the way the Word of God has commanded you to love, how could either of you ever show others that same love or teach others how to obey God's commands? And if others are experiencing the gospel from you, but your spouse is not, that is hypocrisy, and what a destructive force hypocrisy is in the eyes of those who are yet to know God.

"Jesus loves you unconditionally, but my love is totally conditional" is not the message the world should be hearing from your marriage. A marriage after God is one where outsiders would see a reflection of an all-loving Savior in the way a husband sacrificially loves his wife. They would see a humble and submissive church in the way a wife submits in all things to her husband. A marriage after God is salt and light in this world, seasoned with maturity, ripe with good fruit, faithful, and loving above all else.

Is your marriage reflecting the gospel of God's unconditional love and patience, or is it reflecting the false gospel of selfishness and conditional love?

Practice Makes Perfect

When I (Jennifer) was in middle school, one of my favorite classes was woodshop. The smell of sawdust takes me right back to that dusty room with its tools and big metal machines. My woodshop teacher was an older gentleman who reminded me of my grandpa. As we worked on our projects, he would often tell us, "Practice doesn't make perfect. Perfect practice makes perfect."

My teacher was adamant about the importance of perfect work in each step of the process. If I just eye-balled the measuring, skipped the sanding, rushed the cutting, or skimped on the glue, my birdhouse or my shelf would not only look shoddy, but it wouldn't be sturdy enough to serve its purpose, nor would it be anything I could be proud of. Every part of the process to build something great requires time, attention to detail, and an aim for perfection.

How you minister at home is how you will minister to the world. You cannot expect to share the light of the gospel effectively with others if you don't do it at home with your spouse and with your children. Your spouse and your children are gifts from God. The ministry opportunity you have to love them with God's perfect love is the most important ministry you will ever be called to participate in. So ask the Spirit of God to teach you and show you through His Word how He desires you to walk out the first and most important ministry He has gifted to you. By fulfilling your role in this amazing ministry opportunity, God will refine you and mature you, over time assisting you in every other ministry work you put your hands to. This incredible

How you minister at **HOME** is how you will minister to the **WORLD**.

ministry at home will then become the foundation of everything God is building and doing in and through you.

Learning to Cherish and Respect

After that challenging conversation with Matt, we drove home, sobered and serious. In the car we talked about how the conversation had made us feel and how we were going to respond to Matt's challenge.

I (Aaron) told Jennifer that I wanted her to have no doubt in her mind that she is the most cherished woman in the world. I knew my actions toward her would be crucial in helping her to feel cherished, so we discussed practical ways I could cherish her, such as making better eye contact so she knows I am tuned in to her, being more chivalrous, being more gentle in the way I communicate, and expressing my love and desire for her through physical touch without the expectation of sex. Cherishing my wife would require me to be thoughtful of her, thoughtful of her needs, and thoughtful of the ways I can bless her. Although I didn't feel it was in my nature to be a romantic husband, my wife desired that from me. The choice to be a husband who cherished his wife wasn't a hard choice to make; I knew she was worth every effort I could make to cherish her.

I (Jennifer) was just as convicted by that challenging conversation as Aaron was. I always knew I struggled to respect my husband, not because he isn't worth it, but because my natural tendency was toward disrespect. I often would justify my disrespectful behavior toward him by telling myself that my behavior wasn't that terrible, that my feelings were legitimate and therefore I had a right to respond to him the way I did, that I was just made that way, that my responses and interactions were a result of who I was or what I learned growing up. Other times I was completely oblivious to the way I talked to my husband and didn't even notice when I was being disrespectful or unloving.

Now I desperately wanted to change, to grow and mature. I told Aaron how much I truly desired to be the wife God calls me to be by loving and respecting him more. I knew this choice wouldn't be easy. It wasn't a choice to just do more or sprinkle in a few nice comments here and there. I needed to stop a behavior that was extremely natural to me, that had become embedded in my habits because it was first embedded in my heart. I needed this part of my flesh to die.

I promised Aaron that I would pray for God to carve disrespect out of my heart and replace it with a genuine respect for him as my husband. I told Aaron I would strive to practice self-control and be aware of how I was communicating with him. I told him I would be submissive to him in the big and small things to show my love and reverence. And as I shared with him the kind of wife I would be toward him, he smiled, grateful that we were doing this together, moving forward as one for the benefit of both of us and for the message God would radiate through us. We knew our ministry to each other mattered, which encouraged us to make the changes we needed to make.

We can both say now that these choices have made a difference in our relationship. We don't always get it right, but we are committed to cherishing and respecting each other, even in the small things. And those small things make a big difference.

When I (Jennifer) acknowledged Aaron and responded to him with a respectful tone in a situation where I would normally huff, puff, or argue my way through, Aaron noticed immediately and smiled. Or when he would have an idea I didn't agree with, instead of responding with a firm no and then explaining, I would find a way to suggest a better way. I could tell that my position of respect for him affirmed him in a great way. This choice to respect my husband in all things retrained my heart and mind to be thoughtful in the way I addressed him, especially when my emotions were running high. It required self-control, but the more I intentionally practiced respect for him, the more natural it became. For example, in the past when he would leave a used paper towel balled up on the counter instead of throwing it into the trash, I would have said something snarky like, "I really don't care to pick up after two kids today!" I realized that I didn't need to make this such a big deal and that belittling Aaron never led to the solution I desired. So I decided that I would either just throw the paper towel away or I would address the issue by calmly sharing with him how it made me feel.

I (Aaron) also noticed how even the smallest of choices I made to love and cherish my wife made a big difference. For example, I would write on the bathroom mirror with a dry erase marker something like, "I hope you have an incredible day, my love!" She would text me as soon as she saw it to let me know she appreciated my thoughtfulness. Other intentional ways I tried to bless her included opening doors for her when we went out for a date night, complimenting her when I noticed the awesome effort she put toward teaching our son and managing the house, and giving her a foot massage, knowing one of her love languages is physical touch.

The more my wife and I made daily choices to affirm each other in these small ways, the more the atmosphere of our home radiated peacefulness and contentment. The love between us was growing ever more evident. So much, in fact, others started to notice. Our pastor's son, who moved out of state for college, once came home during a holiday and made a comment to his parents about how it seemed that Jennifer and I were even more in love than the last time he saw us. To us this was confirmation that when we walk in God's ways and are obedient to His Word, our marriage reflects His message of reconciliation and love to others.

Although we both have matured over the years, there have been moments we have failed each other, times we were tempted to choose selfishness over serving. At times I (Aaron) lacked gentleness in the way I communicated or neglected to treat my wife in an understanding way. At times Jennifer has reacted to me with disrespect or refused to submit and support me in a decision. Yet, despite these moments of setback, we have grown in our maturity. We now choose to be quick to communicate, sharing with each other how we feel. We are quick to correct our missteps, we are quick to repent when we sin, and we are quick to reconcile. We are practicing perfect holiness as we get better and better with each passing year, learning how to die to our flesh and walk in righteousness. This aim for perfection is building a great big picture of the gospel in our lives as we grow closer to God and closer to each other.

QUESTIONS FOR REFLECTION

1. Husbands: Does your wife feel like she is the most cherished woman in the world?
2. Wives: Would your husband agree that he is the most respected man in the world?
3. Examine your priorities. Are you making your marriage your first ministry? How can you tell?

Chapter 6

WALKING AUTONOMOUSLY
DOESN'T WORK

Only three short years after we made our vows to each other, we found ourselves isolated, severed by brokenness and sin. We were falling apart—not because some marriages "just don't make it" but because our hearts were faint from trying to maintain our marriage our way, instead of submitting to God's way. We were able to get so far down the wrong road, full of sin and negative attitudes about our marriage, because we avoided the very thing God gave to help protect us and keep us going down the right road, His road. We neglected to participate in true community, the fellowship with other believers.

The body of Christ is a gift from God, our source of security and protection. Our marriage relationship would have been fixed and healed more quickly had we chosen sooner to do what we are about to encourage you to do.

For the majority of those early years of marriage, we neglected to rely on the body of Christ—fellow brothers and sisters in the

Lord—to encourage us, advise us, walk with us, and help bear our burdens. We were too prideful to let others know we were struggling, and we were too insecure to let them get to know us that intimately. We also felt an unspoken fear of others knowing about our struggles with sexual intimacy and pornography.

I (Aaron) was ashamed of the sin in my life and how I hurt my wife when I chose to use pornography. My wife, meanwhile, often felt broken or defective because it was her body that was keeping us from enjoying each other. She blamed herself for my addiction to pornography, believing she was a contributing factor for why I kept doing it. My flesh wanted to believe that and often blamed her as well, but deep down, I knew it was my own desire that drove me.

We did not know what it would be like to be fully known. We wondered if we would still be accepted and loved by others, and we wondered what would happen if these dark parts of our hearts and lives were exposed and kept accountable. Even though we knew we should not forsake meeting together with God's people, we were convinced that showing up to church on Sunday mornings with smiles on our faces was sufficient. We snuck into church late and left early. Having moved back home to Southern California after traveling as missionaries, we had very few friends. Many of our older friendships had moved on or were not following God anymore. When we socialized, it was with our extended families.

As we avoided building relationships with other believers, we also began isolating ourselves from each other. We were at the end of our rope, roommates sharing the same space, and we knew that if things didn't change, it would mean the end of our marriage. We didn't possess enough strength or perseverance on our own to hold everything together without God's guidance and help.

Real and Raw

Around this time, by God's grace, I (Aaron) learned about a marriage group meeting at a local church. The group, which met on Wednesday evenings, encouraged married couples to engage in close community and fellowship with each other. I wanted to go as soon as I found out about it, convinced this group would help us, and most likely be our last chance to try and make our marriage work. I invited Jennifer to go with me. It actually took me a few times of inviting her before she agreed to go.

At that time Jennifer was at a low point in her relationship with God, avoiding Him because she was angry for the struggles He was allowing us to experience. Much later she told me, "I felt that if I said no to joining you, it would have been an ultimate *no* to trying to work on our marriage." In Jennifer's mind, this marriage group would be her last effort to find healing in our relationship. To this day, I am extremely grateful for the strength God gave me to persist in inviting my wife to join me and the courage she had to say yes.

That first Wednesday we showed up, we both felt extremely uncomfortable. People seemed so happy to be there, greeting one another and grabbing coffee before finding their seats. Lost in a sea of seemingly well-built marriages, we stood there awkwardly as if a spotlight was shining on us, exposing every crack and crevice in our broken relationship. Could everyone see that our marriage was crumbling? Could they see the financial strain? Could they see my wicked addiction to pornography? Could they see my wife's disdain toward God? Could they see our lack of faithfulness? Could they see that the way we treated each other in front of them was different than the way we treated each other at home? Could they "see" right through us to know all of these things, just by seeing us there that night?

Isn't that exactly how our enemy, the devil, works? The moment we choose to walk in obedience, he's right there to accuse us and remind us of our brokenness and shame, doing everything he can to derail our trajectory toward closeness with God, toward oneness with each other, and toward healing.

Our insecurities and the questions that flooded our minds began to get the best of us. Without even having to communicate, we slowly stepped backward, getting ready to turn around to slip out the doors before the meeting began, hoping to leave before anyone would notice us. But instead of escaping, we met the arms of a man greeting us, inviting us to sit with him and his wife at their table. This couple, Tom and Heidi, made a commotion shuffling chairs and scooting couples around to make room for us.

That night, sitting at that table full of marriages just like ours, we realized we needed this setting more than we could ever have known. We witnessed husbands and wives opening up and talking about their marriages. No masks. No hiding. No faking. Some wept, some laughed, some sat as quietly as we did, hoping not to be called upon. It was real, it was raw, and there was something uniquely appealing about it all. It was refreshing, and that very night hope found its way back into our broken hearts.

A few months later, I (Jennifer) realized I was still avoiding deep intimacy with friends, but I was closer than ever to true change. Tom had invited Aaron to hang out and watch a football game with a few other husbands from our table. Aaron wasn't much of a sports fan, but he has always been a fan of good company and greasy food. I was on my lunch break at work when I saw Aaron's text about his plans for later that evening, and he also encouraged me to spend the evening with Heidi and a few other wives who would be hanging out at the same time that night. And just then, Heidi called to invite me as well.

I immediately apologized for not being able to make it, making up a fake but believable reason for why I was busy. I was nervous about talking with these women, wondering what they would ask me and worried about what I would say. It seemed so much easier to avoid the whole thing. But the Lord convicted my heart in about three seconds. I needed to go spend time with these ladies, but first I needed to apologize for lying. I called Heidi back right away, and she answered on the first ring. My voice shaky from embarrassment, I said, "Hi, Heidi, it's Jen. I am really sorry. I need to tell you that I lied. I said I was busy tonight but I'm not, I was just insecure about coming over."

Heidi chuckled a little and responded, "Really? Why?"

I told her, "I don't know. I think because I don't really have friends, I don't know how to be one. I didn't know what to expect tonight, and it just felt hard to say yes to you. But I actually do want to come, if that's okay?"

"Of course, silly!" she said. Then she gave me the details and her address.

Putting aside my insecurities of what a friendship with Heidi and the other wives would look like or make me feel, I decided to just experience it. That night we all sat around Heidi's big brown leather couch, snacking and chatting. It still wasn't exactly comfortable, but it was exactly what my heart desperately needed.

Tom and Heidi stepped out in obedience to welcome us to the table, and their example of transparency, honesty, and real biblical love inspired us and taught us to walk with the same kind of transparency, honesty, and love. Over the course of two years, God used them, and the other couples at that table, to sharpen us and help restore and mature us. As we spent time with them and built up a friendship, they were able to challenge us. When they pointed out things such as, "Hey, you guys bicker a lot, what's going on?" we knew they were asking because they loved us and wanted to see us grow. When we finally shared our sexual struggles, they challenged us to be intimate with each other, even providing suggestions of ways to make it more fun. Over dinner we would end up confessing sin, crying, and praying together. Finally we understood what Jesus meant when he said, "Love one another: just as I have loved you, you also are to love one another" (John 13:34). This was the love we experienced from our brothers and sisters in Christ.

A Lasting Impact

The redemption and healing we found in our marriage only came once we surrendered to God's way of doing life, which included participating in fellowship with other believers. Our marriage was being transformed by the renewing of our minds about the body of Christ and our place in it. God revealed to us how every person who is a part of His body plays a unique and necessary role, to accomplish His will and purposes. Tom and Heidi, who later became some of our best friends, didn't know at the time how much they would change our lives, but they were faithful in fulfilling the ministry God called them to in their own marriage, and it poured out in their ministry to the other couples there at the table and toward us. Because of their faithful obedience to God, they directly participated in the ministry we are now doing today.

Consider this: If we had continued to avoid the body of Christ, not only would our marriage have been obliterated, but any chance of the ministry that exists in our lives today would have had that same fate. We often think about the impact God has had in tens of thousands of other marriages through our online ministries because of our willingness to rely on Him and His body to help restore our marriage. The ripple of effectiveness our marriages can have when we are submissive to God's ways and reflect His redemption story is unfathomable!

The Power of Unity

There is no such thing as an autonomous Christian who stands alone with no need for others and no obligation to anyone. To be called a Christian, by definition, means being a part of Christ's body, the church. Every Christian must be in fellowship with other believers and is counseled by Scripture to do so. Hebrews 10:24–25 says, "And let us consider how to stir up one another to love and good works, not neglecting to meet together, as is the habit of some, but encouraging one another, and all the more as you see the Day drawing near." Six out of the ten command-ments are directed toward our relationship with others, which in itself is profound. Why would God show us how to walk in love with one another if it was perfectly fine and acceptable for us to avoid deep and meaningful relationships with other believers? He wouldn't. God desires His people to meet together, encourage each other, and love each other.

When Jesus prayed, "Holy Father, keep them in your name, which you have given me, that they may be one, even as we are one" (John 17:11), He was praying for the power of unity as one body with other believers. We, joined together in fellowship with other Christians, are unified in one mission, one heart, and one spirit. As a single body we are called to walk together toward the will of the Father. Our desire is not to please ourselves only, but to please the One who reconciled us to Himself. Fellowship with other Christians is not optional for the Christian, and it is necessary for a healthy, biblical life. A marriage after God recognizes the necessity for godly, biblical Christian fellowship where a husband and wife are known intimately by other believers.

Once we let down our walls of insecurity and began sharing with other Christian married couples what we were facing, we became known. Our struggles became known and our sin became exposed. Through our vulnerability, other Christians were then able to empathize with us, but also offer comfort, suggestions on how to overcome our struggles, and exhortations on repenting and reconciling. When we became known, we felt a deep level of concern and love from these other believers. This affirmed our ability to be transparent. Our experience stripped away the fears of what others would think of us and our anxieties about sharing what we were facing.

Jesus taught us that unity was what the Father's heart is for His people. In John 15:5 He says, "I am the vine; you are the branches. Whoever abides in me and I in him, he it is that bears much fruit, for apart from me you can do nothing." Jesus calls Himself a vine, and He calls us His branches, both of which are pieces of a whole. In nature, there doesn't exist healthy, thriving branches floating around. Rather, what is seen are healthy, thriving branches connected to the main stem of a plant or trunk of a tree, which is rooted with a strong foundation. If there are branches that are found in nature, disconnected and alone, it is either dead or in the process of decaying. In 1 Corinthians 12:27 Paul tells us that we "are the body of Christ and individually members of it." How can we say we are a branch if we are not growing next to other branches? How can we call ourselves members of the body of Christ if we are not connected to the other parts of that same body?

In chapter 2, we talked about Satan's war on our effectiveness. One way he will destroy your effectiveness is to convince you and your spouse to walk in complete autonomy and to hide from other believers. The devil knows that when believers get together and walk together, they will strike blows into his kingdom. Not only that, but as you walk in unity with the body of Christ in community, you become strong and less vulnerable to attack.

We know why people tend to avoid true biblical fellowship, because we used to avoid it too. We know these types of relationships can be messy. We know the possibility and likelihood of hard, uncomfortable conversations. We know that with being known comes accountability, and with accountability comes change, which can be painful. We know that being known can seem terrifying.

However, since experiencing the power of true community and fellowship with the body of Christ, we have come to know so much more of the good that comes from walking this way, in contrast to walking alone and isolated from the body. We know the benefits of iron sharpening iron. We know the intrinsic value of being needed and being provided for. We know the good that comes from being known, and we are no longer afraid of it.

We desire this same knowledge that comes through experience to transform you and your marriage as you and your spouse walk in unity with the body of Christ. Do not be afraid of it. Do not be convinced that you can live without it. Not only is fellowship with other believers an incredible benefit to the refining of your marriage relationship, but it is also where you and your spouse will discover an extraordinary opportunity to serve and love others in Christ through the ministry of your marriage.

Living in Obedience

Here are some thoughts for you to consider as you and your spouse navigate where your marriage lands in the area of fellowship.

Walking in autonomy is not only dangerous for your marriage, it is also rebellious. Our relationship with Christ cannot be separate from our relationship with other believers. Simply going to church on Sundays and saying a quick hello to people you know is not fellowship. True biblical fellowship only happens when you can be fully known by other Christians, and when those same Christians are trusted to speak freely and openly with you about your walk with God, your marriage, your parenting, and so on. Be willing to build up relationships with people at your church by being honest with them, spending time with them, and speaking truth into each other's lives.

Your marriage and the ministry God has for your marriage will only benefit from the obedience of living and walking in true biblical fellowship. Being intimately known and loved by other believers and intimately knowing and loving your brothers and sisters in Christ is exactly what God intended for us as His body. This, in itself, is a ministry, as Jesus himself tells us: "By this all people will know that you are my disciples, if you have love for one another" (John 13:35).

Are you known? Do other believers have permission to speak truth into your life? Are they close enough to you to know how you are walking, thinking, and living so that they can correct you if necessary? Or encourage you? Or help you? Are you and your spouse actively pursuing your roles in the body of Christ by intentionally getting to know those whom you fellowship with, encouraging them, and speaking God's truth into their lives?

Your marriage is an active and necessary member of the body of Christ. Whether or not you and your spouse have been walking in the kind of fellowship that we have discussed in this chapter, today is a new day and today you can actively pursue healthy biblical fellowship and witness for yourselves how God will strengthen, challenge, and empower your marriage for His purposes through your experience of engaging with and being supported by His body. If you are not doing so already, take time to build up strong friendships with Christian couples, people who will sit down over coffee and have a conversation with you about how you can grow in your marriage. Have them over for dinner or serve them in a need they might have. Make yourselves known by sharing your hearts with them. Tell them the things you are struggling with, the things you fear, or the victories you have had. Give them permission to be a part of your life and to speak into your life. Be humble, get to know them, and speak truth into their lives as well. When all the parts of Christ's body are functioning in perfect harmony, nothing will stop the body from accomplishing God's will.

Be **TRANSPARENT** with your marriage, be **HONEST**, and love well.

Don't be like us, hiding from others because of shame and brokenness. Don't be like us, trying to slip out the back door before anyone could see us. Instead, be like those husbands and wives who opened their arms, their hearts, and their homes to welcome others to participate in the extraordinary body of Christ. Don't wait to be pursued; be the pursuers. Don't wait to be served; be the faithful servants. Don't wait to be loved and invited. Love and invite. Be transparent with your marriage, be honest, and love well. We are all connected. We are all one in Jesus Christ, and He is our head, leading us and guiding us to do His will in this world.

QUESTIONS FOR REFLECTION

1. Why is it so important to your marriage that you be vulnerable and real with other Christians?
2. Have there been past moments where others have sought biblical fellowship with you and you did not receive? If so, what kept you from participating?
3. If you do not already enjoy community and accountability with other believers, where might you find it, or how could you create it? Take a step this week toward participating in biblical fellowship.

Chapter 7

A GOOD AND
FAITHFUL STEWARD

n the fall of 2008, we found ourselves in a financial drought. We were only a year and a half into marriage, and up to this point the pain of our sexual intimacy issue had overshadowed any other marital stressor. That is, until the last bit of our savings dried up and my (Aaron's) college loan, which had been deferred for almost two years, now needed to be repaid.

Years before we started our online ministries or wrote any books, we were just a young couple trying to figure out how to survive. When we received the notification that we would have to start paying a set amount every month to the school loan, we were living in a back house on a friend's property in the Thousand Islands area of Eastern Canada. We had only been there a few months, with an indefinite plan to help our friends start a nonprofit organization. It was an exciting project with the goal of raising awareness and funds to pave roads in Africa so that rural villages could have access to the well-drilling equipment needed to get clean water. We had the added benefit of working and living next to a beautiful river. Even though this new adventure was peaceful, appealing, and spiritually rewarding, we found ourselves battling growing bitterness toward each other because of our intimacy issues, with the now added pressures of my school loan payment coming due.

Before long, several more obstacles made us question whether we should stay in Canada. We couldn't get jobs where we were living, the nonprofit status was going to take longer than expected, and the ministry support from family and friends, though generous, was not enough to cover our basic needs. With all of these challenges rising up at once, we were forced to reevaluate our situation.

How could we continue doing ministry for God if we had no money?

God spoke to both of our hearts simultaneously with the same message. The Scripture that pressed most heavily on my (Jennifer's) heart was Romans 13:8: "Owe no one anything, except to love each other, for the one who loves another has fulfilled the law." I didn't want to owe anyone anything except love, and I was convinced that as we built a better financial situation by becoming debt-free, we would be better prepared to do any ministry work God had for us.

Meanwhile, Aaron was convicted by the sobering wisdom of Proverbs 22:7: "The borrower is the slave of the lender." He did not want to be a slave to debt but instead to be free to do the work of God.

One morning I invited Aaron for a walk down by the river. It was overcast, with the crisp fall air blowing in from the water. The leaves were changing into magnificent colors, reflecting the coming season of change for our marriage. We both desired God to use us despite our weaknesses and lack of resources. We were okay with the little we had, if it meant continuing to be missionaries for His sake. But no matter how much we wanted to continue in ministry, we felt even more strongly we should get out of debt first.

As we walked, we shared how Scripture had convicted us. Aaron wanted us to pay off our debt and build up our savings. So I proposed that we move back to California to stay with family until we could be on our own. I missed being near my family and saw this as an opportunity to reconnect with them, as well as to pay off our debt. Thankfully, Aaron agreed.

Later that evening we broke the news to our friends. We also called our parents to arrange plans to come home. Just like that, we packed up our little red Jetta and drove 2,891 miles back to our hometown with a new mission: to become debt-free.

When we arrived in Southern California, we immediately began to search for full-time jobs. The biggest hindrance was the repercussions of the 2008 recession. Thankfully, Jennifer was quickly hired at the Christian preschool where she had worked as an assistant for several years prior to our marriage. However, it took me more than two months to get hired, and that was after I offered to work for that company for free for a few weeks, hoping I would impress them enough to hire me. My sacrifice of time worked, and they did hire me. I finally had a job, using my skills in graphic design and web development at a small firm that created branding and design for other businesses. Having two full-time jobs was a crucial component of our strategy to pay off our debt.

In addition to our full-time jobs, we decided to start a

photography business. On the weekends we shot engagement, wedding, and family photos. Photography was something we both enjoyed and could do together to bring in extra cash.

Paying off my school loan was not as easy as we had hoped it would be. Our budget was extremely tight, and our bank account often empty. However, during this season of our marriage we focused on building a strong financial foundation, confident it could help not only our marriage but also God's kingdom. During this time, God was teaching us the value of money, what His Word says about it, and how to be in control of our finances instead of finances always controlling us.

Money Fights

A survey done by Ramsey Solutions published in February 2018 reported that money is the number one issue married couples argue about.[1] We have definitely had our moments of arguing about money problems. However, as God transformed our hearts and minds toward money, not only did we get out of debt, but the contention around our finances drastically declined. We strongly believe having a healthy, biblical view of finances and being willing to embrace God's perspective on debt and money is a significant part of pursuing a marriage after God.

Through experience, we learned the importance of having control over our finances. The question that often popped into my (Aaron's) head was: Can God use a person or a marriage that is in debt? Absolutely! But a better question is this: is it God's perfect plan for someone's life and marriage to operate in debt?

---

1   https://www.daveramsey.com/research/money-marriage-communication.

Not at all! God has called us all to freedom, and being a slave to debt is not freedom. This pursuit of freedom lit a fire in my heart to aggressively pursue getting out of debt.

Our debt hindered us from continuing in the ministry that we had been doing in Canada. It consumed our thoughts as we stressed about the ways we could pay it down when we had so little to live off of. Even though we both agreed to work on getting out of this debt, the tension of our constant need for more money stirred up irritation. Many times we responded to each other with negative attitudes and tense body language in conversations about money. We fought about the situation we were in, arguing who was at fault for it. Our disunity was dismantling our effectiveness, and we felt it. There was no way we could be a light for God when we felt so dull on the inside. The impact of our financial situation was disrupting our marriage, and we didn't want this to be the case for the future of our relationship or mission of serving God.

Of course, God could have wiped our debt out miraculously if that is what He wanted to do. This was something we often prayed for since we knew that God is all powerful and that He had the means to do so. However, He is also a loving Father who desires that we grow up and become wise and mature men and women. If God had just taken away the debt, we may never have learned to be financially prudent. God desires us to be faithful stewards of the resources He has placed in our possession. This was the lesson He had for us to learn, and we wanted Him to trust us with what He gave to us.

Throughout this learning process we didn't always see eye to eye. But over the course of two years, God taught us three principles about finances that have guided us and made us more effective in the ministry God has called us to, even to this day. As a married couple we had to (1) be on the same page, (2) practice a debt-free lifestyle, and (3) be generous.

Be on the Same Page

In those early years of marriage, we realized very quickly that we were not on the same page when it came to our finances. Although we both desired to be debt-free and could at least agree on that point, there were other areas of tension that slowed our progress to that goal.

Instead of accepting the debt as both of ours, deep down Jennifer felt the debt was solely mine and she shouldn't have to be punished for it by sacrificing things she desired to help pay it off. She wrestled with bitterness over the debt I brought into our marriage. However, now that we were married, we needed to work together to get rid of the debt. The fault for the debt didn't matter since we were now one. The debt was ours—not mine or hers, but ours.

We also had very different points of view when it came to spending, saving, giving, and everything in between. I (Jennifer) was looser with spending money. I lacked wisdom with finances and did not have a healthy habit of saving money. Sometimes, when Aaron told me I couldn't make a certain purchase, especially if it was an inexpensive purchase, I would retaliate with frowns and biting comments. The debt he brought into our marriage was fuel that fed my disrespectful behavior.

When it came to being generous, I rarely gave with a cheerful heart. If Aaron suggested that we bless someone with our money or possessions, I reluctantly agreed with him. I had a difficult time trusting God to provide for us and felt that I had to protect what we had.

I blame my immaturity with spending, saving, and giving on my childhood experiences of being raised in a family that had very little. Aaron, on the other hand, had a better sense of how to manage finances. He paid attention to our budget and made sure our checking account was balanced. He also exhibited more self-control in his shopping.

Not only that, but Aaron is a genuinely generous giver. As soon as he has an idea to bless someone, he tries to figure out the quickest way he can do so. Even when we had nothing, he still found ways to give. Although his motivations were good, at times his generosity became a source of contention.

Although I (Aaron) was a generous person, this was an area of my heart I needed to mature in. God used the conversations and confrontations I had with my wife to learn how to give with wisdom guiding us. However, this took time and wasn't an easy process for us to work through.

With our differences toward money rooted in our hearts and woven through who we were, it felt as if we were fighting with each other daily about finances. Being in different places in our understanding of finances caused division in our relationship. In addition, all of our arguing over money was exhausting. Although we found it stressful to talk about money, it was an area of our marriage we wanted to fix.

God used our financial crisis to draw us back to His Word time and time again. He showed us we needed to be in agreement on how to be good stewards of what He gave us. Neither of us could argue with the Word of God! So it was our desire to be obedient to God that motivated us to agree with each other about finances, including giving and paying down debt. We also discovered that unless we talked openly about our finances and our thoughts and feelings surrounding all of it, then we would inadvertently work against each other.

The state of our finances may have been one of the biggest sources of tension in our marriage, but dealing with it helped us learn how to communicate. Instead of responding in frustration when one of us overspent or wanted to give generously, we worked on presenting a solution. We talked about how to make a better budget, and we strategized ways we could get out of debt faster. The more we persisted in communicating about our finances and praying about it, the more we inched our way to being on the same page. And God was faithful to transform our character and help us understand how to work together on this big goal of becoming debt-free.

Once we were on the same page about where our finances needed to be, we learned how to budget together, how to consult each other on purchases, how to make wise purchases, how to save, how to say no to things we wanted but didn't necessarily need, and how to be generous with what we had, even if it was just a little.

If you and your spouse desire to be used by God, and if you desire to be good stewards of the finances God has given to you, then you both need to be on the same page. Honestly and openly communicating with each other about your finances is how you get on the same page. The more you talk about your fears, your circumstances, your bills, your needs, and your income, the more you both will grasp the reality of where your finances are and where you want them to be. From there you can strategize on how to manage a budget, save, or get out of debt. It is also helpful to talk about how your families of origin and past experiences have shaped your view of money. Through your discussions, you may find that one or both of you need a change of heart in order to become a good steward. Be willing to pray about these things as well. Prayer is an action toward unity that should not be neglected.

Don't let the stress of finances be the reason you argue or fight. Instead, use every opportunity to talk about your finances as a time to practice respectful communication and team building. There is no need to point the finger, blame, or figure out who is at fault for messy financial situations. Instead, focus on your oneness and work together as a team. Support each other and stick to the plan you have agreed on. Be one in the way you budget, spend, save, and give. If one or both of you have a sinful spending habit, repent of it today. Continually remind each other of God's financial wisdom by referring back to His Word often.

Come up with a plan on how you will get your finances in control and keep your family out of debt. What we did was create a simple budget where we broke down everything we needed to spend money on, which included: rent, groceries, gas, phone bill, and anything else that was a necessary expense. Removing the mystery of where our money was going was crucial. We agreed on a $10 allowance per person, per week for things like gum or coffee. We also agreed to limit how much extra money we were spending, and we decided we would discuss any purchase of $25 or more. We also added on our budget a line item for giving, and we prayed about how God wanted us to use that money to practice generosity as a family. Communicating and praying regularly about our finances was and continues to be how we stay on the same page.

A marriage after God is one where the husband and wife

encourage each other to have a right perspective about money. Use your words and your actions to affirm each other. Support each other in the decisions you two make in regard to your finances by following through with the strategies you set out to implement. Celebrate the victories along the way, like getting out of debt. Also, as you and your spouse strive to be faithful stewards of all that God has given to you, take time to discuss ways you could use your finances to honor God by blessing the body of Christ or supporting another ministry that is doing good in this world. With your finances in order, you can then have regular, exciting conversations about what God might want to do through your resources. Let God use your finances to make you and your marriage into something effective and valuable for His kingdom.

Practice a Debt-Free Lifestyle

At last the day came: our school loan was paid off! What a day of celebration that was! Since then, we have agreed to live a debt-free lifestyle. We both recognized how painful it was to pour so much time, energy, and effort toward paying off debt, and we never wanted to be in that position again.

To stay debt-free, we continue to strive to be on the same page. We give each other permission to say no to each other on purchases, we continually communicate about finances, we work hard to contribute where we can, we have a shared bank account that we each have access to, and we keep each other accountable in our spending habits. When we notice that spending is out of balance or if we experience a tighter season, we adjust the budget as needed. Our budget started out based on our bi-monthly pay schedule. Every paycheck we received was accounted for and divided as needed to cover our expenses. We used a simple Excel spreadsheet to show us where each paycheck was going to go. This may seem elementary, but often the simplest things produce the most powerful impact over a lifetime, and it is those very things that often get neglected.

We have found it helpful to remind each other often of our budget and boundaries. We don't use credit cards. We don't use car loans. We save for the things we desire. And one of the most important financial decisions we have made is to be content with what we have. We discovered that our desire for things was being stirred up in response to discontentment. It is amazing how much less you crave or actually need when you obey the words of Hebrews 13:5: "Keep your life free from love of money, and be content with what you have, for he has said, 'I will never leave you nor forsake you.'" Checking our hearts when it comes to spending is an important strategy for us. Doing so helps protect our marriage from dangerously misusing what God has given us.

Living a debt-free lifestyle is a radically different approach to living. If you take a look around, you will notice the government, the college system, and the average American family are all slaves to debt. The idea that debt is acceptable—even that debt is the only way to live—is destructive, as it contributes to unnecessary stress.

We don't want you to live under the burden of debt! God has so much more for you than a life dragged down by money you owe. Cut up the credit cards, stop overspending on things that you don't need, learn to be content with what you have, and practice the virtue of patience. When you change from a debt-acceptance mindset to a debt-free mindset, you will realize, as we did, that you have more than enough to live an abundant life, and that God will take care of you with His gracious provision. Contentment is what we must desire. The reason most debt exists in the first place is because we are not content, because we are not patient, or because we believe a lie that debt will help our current situation. When we take matters into our own hands like this, we are trusting the bank, rather than God, to supply our needs. Don't take away the opportunity from God to answer your prayers of need. Instead, trust Him and encourage your spouse to trust Him by living debt-free.

We challenge you to evaluate your current financial situation, communicate with each other on how you measure up according to God's Word, and if necessary make adjustments so that you are faithfully stewarding all that the Lord has given to you. Don't ever accept the lie that debt is the way to live. Seek to maintain God's perspective.

Paul gives us a very clear and powerful command: "Owe no one anything, except to love each other" (Romans 13:8). It is easy to look at this verse and say simply, "Paul really wants us to love others." But that's not the whole concept being shared here. Paul is telling us that the only thing we should be in debt to is loving other people. In fact, we will be able to love more freely and more extravagantly when we do not have obligations to debt. Let this call to love others be our motivation to never cease chasing after a debt-free lifestyle.

Be Generous

When we were paying off our debt, I told Jennifer, "I don't want us to wait to give until we are debt-free; we need to give now. We need to be generous with what we have, and we need to make our account available to God to use for His purposes." We already tithed faithfully, but I also wanted to give above and beyond ten percent. I shared with her Hebrews 13:16: "Do not neglect to do good and to share what you have, for such sacrifices are pleasing to God."

God does not want us to value our money or possessions more than Him, each other, or others, all whom we have been called to love. We experienced firsthand what happens when we put money or possessions on a pedestal. Every time we cared more about money or things than we cared about each other, we fought. It was a destructive behavior that I knew would destroy our marriage if we let it. I was convinced God wanted us to open our hands and release the grip we had so tightly on the money we had in our possession and see it all as His. I had a vision for our marriage. I saw us as people who were generous, people who wanted to be a blessing to God and to others.

We needed to be able to say, "Okay, Lord, you've blessed us, and we want to be a blessing with whatever it is we have; even if it is our last penny." We had to refuse the lie that we couldn't be generous until we had more to give. If we waited to be generous, we wouldn't have exercised our giving muscles. We would have continued to believe that we needed more in order to give.

Remember the story about the woman who gave her last two coins to the temple? Jesus pointed her out to His disciples and said, "This poor widow has put in more than all those who are contributing to the offering box. For they all contributed out of their abundance, but she out of her poverty has put in everything she had, all she had to live on" (Mark 12:43–44). Jesus was declaring that giving is not about quantity but rather about the motives of the heart. Our motives matter. If our hearts are to please God and fulfill His purposes, we must operate with a conviction that what we have belongs to Him.

In our marriage, we had to change from believing the money we had was ours to believing it was all God's and trusting Him with it. One way God revealed to us the importance of checking our motives when it came to money was through a selfish decision I (Aaron) made in the midst of striving to get out of debt. I wanted to purchase a $300 paintball gun. I spent months researching the one I would buy, convinced that owning one would make me feel better, because in the past I felt successful being on a paintball team. Not only that, but I believed paintball would provide me a reprieve from the turmoil in our marriage and the endless hours of work. Although I was seemingly eager to put every penny we earned toward paying down my school loan, I somehow managed to justify this expensive hobby. Unfortunately, I bought the paintball gun, but it sat, unused, on the floor of our bedroom for four months. I only ever used it one time.

Looking back on that terrible purchase, which we were not in any position to support, I regret it. Yet, I am thankful for the experience and what God revealed to me through it. I learned the value of checking my motives, submitting my desires to God, and asking Him for wisdom. Had I submitted my plans to God, He may have pointed out that a paintball gun could not cure what ailed me, and He could have showed me how to spend that money more wisely.

This was not the only time I have used money selfishly. My wife and I both have had our moments of weakness and selfishness. We had to learn that our selfish desires will never be satisfied, whether we make purchases to fulfill a desire or not. We both would attest that the only way we have ever been truly satisfied with our finances is when our finances are in order according to God's Word, when we let Him lead us in how to spend and give, and when we communicate openly with each other, giving room for the other person to speak words of wisdom as we navigate purchases together.

We were learning that the motives of the heart matter. Jesus said, "Do not lay up for yourselves treasures on earth, where moth and rust destroy and where thieves break in and steal, but lay up for yourselves treasures in heaven, where neither moth nor rust destroys and where thieves do not break in and steal. For where your treasure is, there your heart will be also" (Matthew 6:19–21). We had to change what we treasured in order to change our attitude and behavior with money. We had to treasure God's will for our life and marriage above anything money could ever buy.

Being aware of the motives of our hearts and regularly checking ourselves became an important part of the process of learning to be faithful stewards. We asked each other why we wanted to spend money on certain things and why we wanted to give, making sure we had a godly perspective leading us.

As I (Aaron) searched God's Word for that godly perspective on our resources, I found Scriptures that encouraged us to give generously. Acts 20:35 says, "We must help the weak and remember the words of the Lord Jesus, how he himself said, 'It is more blessed to give than to receive.'" And 2 Corinthians 9:6–7 says, "Whoever sows sparingly will also reap sparingly, and whoever sows bountifully will also reap bountifully. Each one must give as he has decided in his heart, not reluctantly or under compulsion, for God loves a cheerful giver." Whenever we were made aware of a need, we would pray to see if God wanted us to help, and if so, how. We wanted the money God had given us to not just benefit us but also others who God put in our path. We carved out time in our schedule to share with each other any concerns we may have had and took the time to truly listen, reaffirming good communication practices in our marriage.

Becoming generous people did not come easy to us. This has been an area of continual growth for us as a couple as we look to Scripture to guide us. We are encouraged by Proverbs 11:24–25, which says, "One gives freely, yet grows all the richer; another withholds what he should give, and only suffers want. Whoever brings blessing will be enriched, and one who waters will himself be watered." Thankfully, we are growing in our agreement on finances. Whether or not we ever grow financially richer, we believe in the promises of God. Together, we fight our flesh to practice being generous as a couple and build up that muscle of giving.

We would like to share an opportunity God used in our life to test our hearts toward money and our trust in Him. For two years, working around our full-time jobs, we had been faithfully serving other marriages with daily encouragement through our blogs. We didn't want to distract readers from the content by having ads pop-up in the sidebar, a common way for bloggers to make money on their sites. Of course, without ads we were not gleaning revenue from our sites, despite all the work we were investing into them. As we rounded our third year of blogging, we decided to try selling T-shirts to support our online ministries. Hoping to spread some positive messages about marriage, we designed T-shirts with big, bold text that said, "I love my husband" and "I love my wife." To our surprise and delight, within a few weeks we had sold hundreds of shirts. But rather than using the money for ourselves as we had planned, we felt a growing urge to give all the money we made from those sales back to God.

Ultimately, we agreed that we would give God this first lump sum as an offering. We wanted to demonstrate our thankfulness for the success of the shirt campaign, as well as our gratitude for how many couples God was reaching through our blogs. We wanted to give it to God to practice trusting Him, believing that if He could trust us with this money, He could trust us with more. We also saw this as an exercise to teach our flesh to be submitted to God in finances so that we would not be controlled by money. No matter how much money we had, we wanted to be open-handed and cultivate a heart of generosity.

We began to pray and ask the Lord how He desired the money to be used and we asked Him where He wanted it to go. A few days later God revealed to us a few significant needs, showing us who we could support with the money from the selling of those shirts. We could have easily justified keeping that money for ourselves. We could have negotiated down how much we would give and how much we would keep. But I repeat: Giving this money was our way of telling our flesh who we serve, and telling God that we trusted Him to keep providing for our needs.

It is never convenient or easy to give money or to be generous with other resources, such as time or energy. Our flesh will squirm at the thought of selfless living. But the example of Christ, His sacrifice and His teaching, motivates our hearts to give. We never give out of compulsion; rather, we give out of a heart to please God, to bless others, and to train our hearts and minds not to serve money. Through our experience of faithfully stewarding all that the Lord has given to us, we have grown to

A MARRIAGE after God is MARKED by generous living.

understand the significance of giving generously and how God can use our finances in ways that impact His kingdom for good. We have had the blessing of seeing His work fulfilled in the lives of others, and it humbles us to know we get to participate in that.

Generosity is a biblical principle that God desires His people to live out. Search His Word and meditate on the teaching He provides about being generous. Let His Word lead you and your spouse to be good givers and serve as the motivation for giving generously. Remember that the motive of the heart matters. Being generous is not about how much you and your spouse give and it is not about what you give; being generous is about *why* you give! A marriage after God is marked by generous living.

The Goal of Generous Living

A marriage after God is no slave to debt! A marriage after God is known by the husband and wife's generosity, richness in good works, and the way they trust the Lord every day of their lives. A marriage after God intentionally builds a healthy, biblical financial foundation. A husband and wife who desire to follow God's ways and not the world's ways when it comes to money will know His heart on the matter. They study His Word, they know it well, they manage their finances based on His principles, and they are more concerned with storing their treasure in heaven, because that is where their hearts are.

Money comes and goes. Financial strains come and go. Possessions come and go. This life is temporary and brief. We cannot waste time arguing about finances or fighting for what we think we deserve because we work hard for our money. You and your spouse are a gift to each other. We urge the two of you to increase your unity by working together, being on the same page with each other, living a debt-free lifestyle, and being generous people. Be a light in this dark world, showing others that money is not your master, but God is!

Do you and your spouse have a tight grip on your finances? Does your financial situation control you as it dictates other areas of your life? If your answer is yes, we encourage you to open up your hands and hearts to God, letting go of that tight grip you have had on your finances. Trust God with everything you have, because the reality is that God can do so much more with it than you could ever imagine. Joyfully anticipate and prepare to participate in every opportunity God brings your way to support His purposes.

We don't want you to experience the burden of feeling like you are failing, we don't want you to be overwhelmed by debt, and we don't want you to feel like you are controlled by your financial situation, rather than being in control of it. If this is what you choose to walk out and practice in your marriage, you will be ineffective in your marital ministry and you will be unprepared to financially support His purposes.

The choice is yours. Not yours by yourself and not only your spouse's choice, but how the two of you walk this out together. The choice is yours.

Perhaps you are reading this right now and think your financial foundation is established because you are wealthy. Maybe you and your spouse already live a debt-free lifestyle. If this is the case, then you are off to a great start! Well done! However, we must also direct your heart to what Scripture tells those that are wealthy so that you may evaluate your financial situation and the condition and motives of your heart, to prepare for the opportunities God has for you to financially support His will,

His work, and His purposes. Paul had this advice for Timothy when dealing with the rich: "As for the rich in this present age, charge them not to be haughty, nor to set their hopes on the uncertainty of riches, but on God, who richly provides us with everything to enjoy. They are to do good, to be rich in good works, to be generous and ready to share, thus storing up treasure for themselves as a good foundation for the future, so that they may take hold of that which is truly life" (1 Timothy 6:17–19).

The goal for every marriage after God is to build a healthy and biblical financial foundation so as to be good stewards and good servants with everything God entrusts to us. You and your spouse must long for the Master, your heavenly Father, to say, "Well done, good and faithful servant" (Matthew 25:21). Strive to obey the Word of God and to follow the wisdom He provides about finances. Consider the impact your marriage can make in God's kingdom if you manage faithfully what He has given to you. Now, with your finances in order, imagine how much more He can trust you with.

QUESTIONS FOR REFLECTION

1. Are you on the same page when it comes to your finances? If not, what is one thing you can do to address that problem?
2. Why is it important to pursue a debt-free life and mindset?
3. Why is it important to be generous? How can you be more generous this week with your time, money, or resources?

Part 3

WHAT'S IN YOUR TOOL BELT?
THE EQUIPMENT

Chapter 8

OUR TOOL BELT

n February 2011 we sent the last $1,000 payment to completely wipe out the balance of our debt. With this milestone behind us, we were eager to pursue God's will for the next stage in our lives.

We were both working full-time jobs, but Aaron had been encouraging me to start blogging, confident that writing would be a great outlet for me and help me process all of the growth we had been experiencing in our marriage. For months we talked about this blog having the potential to encourage other wives as well. The more time we spent discussing this purpose of my blog, Aaron realized he also had a desire to have a site that would encourage men in their role as husbands. In fact, it quickly became evident that both sites were necessary to demonstrate what a biblical marriage looks like.

The blog sites were not officially launched just yet. They were ready, but I wasn't quite ready. As this idea of blogging about our marriage became a reality, my nerves spiked and I wrestled with a few insecurities. What would people think of me? Would they make fun of us? Would they leave negative comments? What if they started asking us difficult questions we were not prepared to answer? Was our story good enough to share, or would I be wasting my time? Although I was convinced my blog would be an encouragement for other wives, doubts and fears plagued me.

But as we put the final touches on UnveiledWife.com and HusbandRevolution.com, God revealed to us something that calmed my heart. He showed us that we were able to pursue this ministry because He had been equipping us with the experience and skills to get the work done. It was awesome to look back over the years and see how each of our experiences had prepared us for this new ministry.

Honing Our Skills

In the early years of our marriage, we were traveling overseas with limited ability to connect with family. So we decided to make a website that would host our monthly newsletter, where we would update our family and friends on our adventures and the wonderful work God was doing through us. This had been our very first experience with a blog, even though we didn't call it that. Every month for the first two years of our marriage, we updated our site with photos and descriptions of our work. We shared prayer requests and ministry opportunities. This small, digital newsletter was our first website. It wasn't elaborate by any means, but it was ours, and we loved being able to share in this capacity.

That same year, in 2007, we also self-published and self-printed our very first book with the help of a friend who worked at a local scrapbooking store. We had an idea to combine Aaron's photography archive from his first trip to Africa with some of my poetry to make a book that we would take with us when fundraising for our next mission trip. We gave them away at churches for a suggested donation as a way to raise funds for our next trip to Africa.

A few years later, we built a website for our photography business and began to use social media to connect with potential clients. We updated our photography blog weekly with the best photographs we had taken of engaged couples, families, and weddings, sharing them on Facebook in an effort to book more shoots.

During this season of our marriage, I (Aaron) had several jobs that helped sharpen my skill set in email marketing, web coding, and graphic design. My previous positions with missionary organizations, churches, a Christian retailer, and several small internet-based businesses would add the experience we needed to create our blogs. Meanwhile, to hone her skills, Jennifer took community college classes in photography, creative writing, and Photoshop. At the time we were pursuing these things to help us in our photography business, not realizing we were also acquiring skills that would later help us to be successful bloggers and authors.

Our understanding of how God uses different parts of our lives, what we have experienced and learned along the way, has grown tremendously. God used each one of these jobs and learning opportunities to help us with what we are doing today. Nothing has been a waste.

To this day, whenever we encounter a new opportunity, learn something new, or gain a new skill, we remind each other that God is filling up our tool belt for the purposes He has for us. This affirms our hope for the future—that no matter what happens, we are confident about serving God together as a team for the rest of our lives.

Using Our Experiences

Not only did God use the skills we acquired during our early years of marriage, He also used our experiences. The first four years of our marriage were tough. We experienced trials we never imagined we would have to face. Not only did we encounter frustrations in the bedroom, but we also had to learn how to live on next to nothing, how to reconcile after we sinned against each other, and how to communicate. These difficult issues strained our marriage and stirred up negative feelings about the journey we were on. The more bitter and angry we felt about our situation, the more we became convinced that divorce was our only solution.

In *The Unveiled Wife*, I (Jennifer) recount a pivotal moment in our marriage. I was sitting in church, wondering if our marriage was going to end. It was a devastating time for both of us. Aaron had just told me how deeply depressed he was concerning our relationship, and I thought that if he didn't have anything left to give, no words to encourage us to keep going, no hope in his eyes to affirm me, then he had already made up his mind that we needed to move on.

I (Aaron) was sitting next to my wife, my head hung low. I couldn't quite hear what the pastor was teaching because of the thoughts running through my head. *What should we do? Nothing seems to be working. Is it her fault? Is it mine? Why can't we just be normal? Are we supposed to just divorce? God, I can't live like this anymore. I don't know what to do.*

As I called out to God amid my doubt and frustration, I felt the Holy Spirit speak to me. He brought me all the way back to the garden of Gethsemane. I'm sitting there in the garden, and I see Jesus there, weeping and praying. He cries, "Lord, may this cup pass my lips." Then He says, "Not my will, but Yours be done." I'm watching this play out in my head, remembering the story from Luke 22, and I see that the groom, Jesus, knows exactly what He is about to endure for His bride, the church. He is asking God for a way out, so He won't have to experience the torture of the cross and separation from His Father. The suffering he faces is unimaginable. It is too much. But Jesus's actions reflect the love in His heart. He chooses to obey and submit to His Father's will.

In that moment in the garden, Jesus chose the Father's will to be done, not His own.

In my marriage, I felt like what we were going through was too much. I felt like giving up. But remembering Jesus in the garden, I prayed, "Okay, God, if this suffering is something I have to deal with in my marriage, I will do it anyway."

In that moment sitting in church, I chose God's will for my marriage, not my own.

My wife and I did not speak about divorce that day. Instead, I repented of my hopelessness and bad attitude. I reassured Jennifer that I would love her no matter what, even if we could never have sex or if life wasn't the way we wanted it to be. As I told her how sorry I was for not loving her unconditionally, her eyes filled with tears, and she bowed her head to wipe them away. But I needed her to see me, to see my heart, and to know this was real. So I pulled her closer and with trembling fingers gently guided her gaze up to mine. Then I told her I would always be faithful to her and that I wasn't going anywhere.

This story is a testimony, Jesus's testimony in my life of His patience with me. Jesus showed me that He too had struggled and suffered when He took on all the sin of the world. I only had to take on a little bit of my wife's and my struggles. If Jesus could endure, I could endure. His testimony empowered me and gave me hope for our future together.

That story is a tool in our tool belt. That testimony is not of my ability or my power or my strength; it is absolutely and only Jesus's. It was Jesus Himself coming to me, through the Holy Spirit, and telling me, "Hey, if I can do it, you can too." It changed everything. It changed my whole perspective on my marriage. And now I stand before groups of couples sharing this story with tears in my eyes, and it brings tears to their eyes too, because there is power in the testimony of Jesus.

Together, Jennifer and I mustered up enough courage to keep our faith in the plan God had for us, and He was faithful to transform our hearts. God reconciled our relationship, eventually healing even our intimacy issue. God also helped set me free from my addiction to pornography—but that is a story to tell another time.

These experiences were not something we asked for. It's not like we told God, "Hey, we want to have a marriage blog; let's have a horrible marriage and then make up." There is no way a blog or best-selling book or anything else would ever be worth the hardship we encountered in those first years of marriage. We didn't want our marriage to start out that way, but it did. The hardship we endured became a part of our story that God invited us to share for His glory.

Building the Kingdom

Finally, on March 11, 2011, we launched Unveiled Wife and Husband Revolution. We submitted our desires for these two blogs to the Lord and allowed Him to lead us as we shared our story with hope in our hearts to bring Him glory.

Since launching these blogs, as well as the Marriage After God podcast, we have had many conversations about the journey God has taken us on. Nothing has been a waste. God has used every hardship in our marriage, every victory, our finances, our skills, our talents, our experiences, our relationships with others—all to fulfill His purposes in furthering His kingdom. He has used us to draw others closer to Himself.

We never would have expected to host blogs, be the coauthors of over eleven books, be mentioned in *Publisher's Weekly*, and be listed on the Amazon best-seller list. When we think about it, we are still in awe. When we consider the journey we have been on, we see how God has intentionally filled our tool belt with the things we need to do the work He has called us to today.

A home builder doesn't show up to build a house without his tools. In fact, he comes prepared, wearing his tool belt, where everything he needs to build is in reach, and he is confident in how to use his tools to accomplish the work set before him. He has the blueprints in his hand and is eager to make progress for the purpose of building a home.

As believers, we are all like the home builder, although our mission is kingdom focused. We have acquired skills and experiences and are now eager to work as unto the Lord, doing whatever He has for us to do. Just as God has led us on a journey with specific work to do, your marriage is also on a journey toward the extraordinary work God has prepared for only the two of you to do.

In the next two chapters we are going to take a closer look at how God has made your marriage unique, and we are going to define what makes up your marriage tool belt, the very things God has equipped you with to fulfill the extraordinary work you will accomplish for Him.

QUESTION FOR REFLECTION

How does it help you to know that nothing is ever wasted—that God will use everything in your life to fulfill His purposes for you and your marriage?

Chapter 9

YOUR MARRIAGE IS UNIQUE

Maybe you are looking at the details of our life shared in the last chapter, how each and every piece fit together so intricately to build what has now become our ministry, and you are saying to yourself, "Well, maybe if we did and experienced everything you did, we would be able to have a ministry like that too." Or perhaps you are thinking more along the lines of "Well, we can't do that; we don't have those skills or resources or experiences like you do, and we never will." If you were entertaining these types of thoughts, here would be our response to you:

"Exactly!"

Your marriage is *not* our marriage. You and your spouse are *not* us. You don't have our experiences, talents, education, or upbringing. The beauty of the body of Christ is that each and every part is unique, your marriage included, and God will use your uniqueness for His purposes, if you let Him. God does *not* want another Aaron and Jennifer Smith; He wants you and He wants your marriage!

The **BEAUTY** of the body of Christ is that each and every part is **UNIQUE,** your marriage included.

God is not pleased with us simply because of how big or successful our ministry might look on the outside. His use of us is not made possible because of how "skillful" and "affluent" our lives might be. God isn't saying to the angels in heaven, "Now look there; Aaron and Jennifer are so talented and special. I can surely use them to do something amazing in this world." No!

God's heart is the same for us as it is for you, and His will for your life and marriage is that you would do exactly the same thing that He has called all of His children to do: to love Him and serve Him with all your heart, soul, strength, and mind (Luke 10:27). He desires you and your spouse to be wholly devoted to Him. He wants your unique history and experiences, He wants your unique talents and gifts, He wants your creativity and resources, and He wants your marriage and all that goes with it, to be yielded to Him fully and completely, so that He can show the world who He is through you and your spouse.

Think of your life and marriage like this: everything you have, everything you've been through, all the secret and public things that have happened to you, your every thought and idea, your every skill and talent, all of the education, resources, emotions, and everything else are all God's! He either has allowed them to happen or has given them to you to steward for Him; you are His beloved servant and God is the Master who owns them all. What you have been given is exactly what you need to do exactly what God wants. We want you to hear the words "Well done, good and faithful servant." This is what we desire to hear when we stand before our Father in heaven. This is the prize we are chasing after.

So then, comparison is no longer even a question. Yes, the temptation will always be there to look to the right and left and feel other couples have it far more "together" than you do—but don't let "highlight reels" on social media deceive you. God has qualified you precisely for the ministry of *your* marriage. No one else can fulfill what your marriage can, because your marriage is unique! You don't have to get caught up in the comparison trap anymore. In fact, God is calling you not to. Comparison will rob you of the joy and blessing of serving God. Comparison is the enemy's trap to distract you from keeping your eyes on the prize.

There will be times you get discouraged because other couples can seemingly do more for God because they have been given more than you. Don't rule you or your spouse out of the responsibility of participating. The truth is that you are responsible for stewarding all that God has given you, whether it be much or little, whether you think it is enough or not, and it is your responsibility to submit it all to God and pray about how He wants to use your marriage to serve Him. Then it is a matter of committing your marriage to the work that He is inviting you to do.

It can be very easy to look at your lives, marriage, home, job, or anything else that you have and believe that you are not enough or that these things are standing in the way of what God wants to do. It can be easy to desire more than you have or something different than what you have been given. To desire more would be discontentment, and to desire what someone else has would be coveting. God already knows what you need, and He also knows what you desire. Second Peter 1:3 affirms God's love and provision for you, declaring, "His divine power has granted to us all things that pertain to life and godliness, through the knowledge of him who called us to his own glory and excellence." You and your spouse already have everything you need;

it is found in the knowledge of Jesus Christ. What God desires more than anything from your marriage is that your hearts be submitted to His will and that you choose to walk in obedience to His Word every single day.

Your marriage in the hands of the almighty God is like clay in a potter's hands. The clay cannot say to the Potter, "Why have you made me like this?" (Romans 9:20). The Great Potter loves His creation to be pliable and willing to be used however He sees fit. Trust His work in your life and marriage. Trust His will and direction. Seek what He has for you and the uniquely designed life and marriage that He has given to you to steward for His glory.

So, what are all the things that make up the uniqueness of your marriage? How can you identify and apply all of the tools God has given you so that you can steward them well? In the next chapter we will walk you through the four areas where God has equipped you and your marriage for the unique purpose He is leading you toward.

QUESTIONS FOR REFLECTION

1. Why is comparing ourselves to other couples so dangerous and destructive?
2. Do you currently, or have you in the past, disqualified yourselves from serving God because you felt unqualified or unequipped?

Chapter 10

WHAT'S IN YOUR TOOL BELT?

Think about it like this: your marriage tool belt is like a wedding gift from God. It is a sturdy belt, meant to bind the two of you together, so that you work together as one, a team for His glory. It has pockets and compartments for you and your spouse to fill up. Some of its contents will be made up from your past, because those things contributed to who you are today. However, most of the room is for the two of you to compile as you live your lives together. Your marital tool belt is unique to the two of you, and through it God will do extraordinary works for His kingdom. Remember that nothing is ever wasted. God will use all that you have and all that you have been through, if you let Him.

So what's in your tool belt? We have identified four key areas that make up the "tools" in your belt: (1) your experiences, (2) your testimonies, (3) your natural gifts and talents, and (4) your resources. These four tools will determine how God leads you and your spouse to help build His kingdom.

#1 Your Experiences

The first thing in your tool belt is your experiences. Everything you have encountered in life, everything you have been through and anything that has been done to you is experience. This includes conversations you have engaged in, conflicts you have persevered through, relationships you have had, jobs you have held, camps or conferences you have been a part of, churches you have attended, educational opportunities you have had, skills you have learned, countries where you have traveled, and any other life event you have participated in.

Experience will equip you for what you will encounter as you pursue ministry. Your past experience will help you navigate present trials or difficult situations. Experience will help you complete a job that requires certain skills. It will even help you build connections as you share your experiences with others. No matter what you feel God is calling you and your spouse to pursue, He will use your experience in some way.

Take time to consider your unique experiences. They might be painful, or they might be joyful. Consider the way you were raised, obstacles you've overcome, places you've been, or things you have learned. Perhaps you've dealt with illness or abuse or addiction. These experiences, whether good or bad, will be used by God for His purposes if you allow them to.

Your spouse also has unique experiences. Make it a priority to discuss some of the most significant experiences you both have walked through and dream about how God might use these experiences as a tool to build up His kingdom.

#2 Your Testimonies

The second thing in your tool belt is your testimony. Every Christian has a testimony of how Jesus captured their heart and transformed their life or even their marriage. If you and your spouse confess that Jesus is your Savior and Lord, then you both have testimonies. This rich and powerful part of your tool belt is not so much about you as it is about God. The testimonies you each have detail how you came to know God and how God has changed your life and marriage for the better. Your testimonies attest to the power of Jesus, to the good news of His coming, death, and resurrection.

It requires vulnerability and authenticity to share, "Hey, this is what I've been through, and this is the power of God in my life . . ." Our testimonies have impact because they invite people to learn more about God. When you share your testimony, you are confessing and proclaiming, "Jesus did this for me." A testimony of the gospel glorifies and magnifies the name of God. And when we remember what Jesus has done for us, we are motivated to do good works and share God's love with others.

The testimony is what God has done or is doing in your life and marriage. Whether the tool is used as motivation to complete a job or is used in the midst of working with others, ultimately the way you build God's kingdom is by helping turn hearts toward Him. Also, your testimony will encourage you when the work you are doing is difficult. When the mission you are pursuing is strenuous, when strength is depleting, or hope is fading, a testimony of His work in your life will increase your faith and help you persevere.

#3 Your Gifts

The third tool we have identified in your tool belt is your natural gifts and talents. God put great thought and care into creating you. He knit you together in your mother's womb, knowing before you were born who you would be and the abilities you would have (Psalm 139). He also knew the gifts you and your spouse would have as a team. You and your marriage are no accident! He created both you and your spouse intentionally, with a specific purpose in mind!

Don't let the temptation of comparison draw you away from doing the things God wants you to do. For example, if you have a desire to sing, but you don't sound anything like a platinum recording artist, that doesn't mean you can't still use your gift for God's glory. Or, if you are passionate about photography, yet the industry is chock full of talented photographers, that doesn't mean you should avoid using your gift of photography.

There are millions of people in this world and millions of gifts. It's not about the world's standard of perfection; it's about what's in the tool belt that God has given you and if you are willing to use it. The purpose is not for your notoriety anyway; it is for the glory of God. Take time to identify what your gifts are and don't be afraid to use them!

You are naturally talented at something, and perhaps you have even practiced many hours to excel in those gifts. These talents and gifts come in varying shapes and sizes. There is no master list of all the various gifts, but here are a few to give you an idea of what we mean: organizing, leading, speaking, serving, cooking, teaching, playing an instrument, writing, designing, coding, running a business, caring for children, and so on. There

Don't let the **TEMPTATION** of comparison **DRAW YOU AWAY** from doing the things God wants you to do.

are an enormous number of and a wide variety of gifts. You will most likely discover what your talents and gifts are by identifying what you are passionate about and what you naturally do well.

We know people who excel at doing makeup and hair, and they use their passion in that industry to reach young women who have poor body image. They share with those sitting in their chairs or those who are learning the trade how they have been made in God's image and how God loves them. This is the beauty in God giving everyone different gifts. His love is spread!

We have a friend who was passionate about rock climbing and gifted in business, so he opened a rock-climbing gym. Through his gym he hosted a jacket drive to benefit the homeless. He also led a Bible study at the gym once a week, inviting climbing members to join. His climbing gym is an example of someone building God's kingdom while using a personal gift.

When you married your spouse, you became one. You have been joined together, which means you and your spouse have the opportunity to consider how God can use your individual gifts paired together. The experience of discovering and navigating how to use your gifts as a team for God's purpose is an intimate, affirming, and extraordinary adventure. Have fun figuring out how to use your gifts and passions to spread the good news about Jesus.

Natural talents and gifts are amazing tools God can use in your life for His glory. It may be that you have a special interest or passion in your tool belt that you just never thought God would use, or maybe it is something that does not seem to have anything to do with the Gospel. Yet, what if God is prompting you, saying, "I gave you that for a reason and there's a powerful thing I'm going to do with it, if you let Me." How will you respond to His call?

#4 Your Resources

The fourth and final tool in your tool belt is your resources. This includes your personal relationships, money, time, education, location, material possessions, or any other assets that you can draw from to do any work God calls you to do. Material possessions may include but are not limited to: computers, cameras, books, food, home, car, tools, and so on. God wants you to use these resources to build His kingdom.

It is important to take inventory of our resources and give God permission to use them. If you have a large business network, perhaps you can help someone in their job search. If there is a nearby pregnancy resource center, perhaps you and your spouse can volunteer your time there or provide for specific needs of the fathers and mothers whom they purpose to serve. If you and your spouse have a home, maybe God wants you to open it up to welcome others to your table for food and fellowship. These are just a handful of ideas to get you brainstorming on how God may want to use your resources to serve His people and His purposes.

God Is Already at Work!

The work of God's ministry and the way in which His kingdom is built happens in many different ways. God wants to use you to do good for His purpose. He has equipped you and your spouse with experiences, testimonies, gifts, and resources in order to carry out the work He has called you to do. Our hope in sharing this is to expand your vision of how God can use you and your spouse. We hope knowing what's in your marriage tool belt helps you see what God is calling you and your spouse to do and how the two of you can do it effectively.

The truth is that God is already doing incredible things in this world, and He is inviting you to join Him!

QUESTIONS FOR REFLECTION

1. What experiences have you had, both individually and as a couple, that may be useful in building God's kingdom?
2. What is your testimony; how has God shown His work in your life?
3. What are your gifts and talents, and how might they be used by God?
4. What are some resources you have that you can share?

Part 4

DREAMING TOGETHER:
THE APPLICATION

Chapter 11

TAKE INVENTORY

You may be reading this with your spouse by your side, considering this concept of a tool belt. You can see the different types of tools that fill your belt, and you feel deep in your heart this tugging, like you are being commissioned to build something great. But, even with this tool belt in your hands, you are wondering if you have what it takes to complete the work. Maybe you are questioning whether you are actually qualified to even use the tools. Or perhaps you are looking at the tools, thinking they are not good enough to get the job done, or you are not skilled enough to use them. You might be feeling like you just don't have enough of what you need to keep going. Maybe you and your spouse are sitting there wondering . . . *can we really do this?*

Don't worry, these considerations and insecurities are a normal part of the process. We are finite humans, but what empowers us is our belief in the infinite provision of God and His faithfulness. You have everything you need to fulfill the purpose God has for you. You are qualified and you are good enough—not because you have been credentialed but because the living Holy Spirit empowers you. The tools you have to work with are good enough because God chose you to have them, and He desires you to use them.

You have all that you need to keep going because God is supplying you through His faithfulness, just as a father provides for his children. God is a good Father and He loves you very much! He is commissioning you to build your marriage on His Word, He is commissioning you to build up His body, and He is commissioning you to build your life in such a way that it is a lighthouse set on a hill, a beacon of hope to guide the lost back to Him. Of course you have what it takes to build this for Him! Trust the Commissioner Himself to give you what you need to get the work done. He has already counted the cost of the build, He is all in, and He is ready to guide you through it.

The tools God has given to you and your spouse are unique for the work He desires you to do. Becoming familiar with each tool in your tool belt, examining them closely, and knowing how to use them will make you a good builder. When insecurity overwhelms you, when doubt creeps into your mind about not being good enough to accomplish the work—that is when trusting God and having faith in Him will help you persevere. Walk humbly with the Lord as He leads you and resist the temptation to bury your tool belt when fear bombards you. Go back to the blue prints, the manual for life, which He has already provided. Dig into His Word, and there you will find encouragement for your heart.

Trust in God During Challenging Times

You are not alone in feeling insecure or fearful when it comes to doing the good work that God has commissioned. A story in 1

Kings 17 about a poor, starving widow can remind you to trust in God during challenging times.

In a time of severe drought and famine, God tells the prophet Elijah to go to Zarephath, where he will find a widow who will feed him. When Elijah meets this widow, he asks her to bring him a morsel of bread. The widow explains that she does not have any bread, only a handful of flour and a small amount of oil, hardly enough for her and her son to live on, let alone to share with a stranger. In fact, the famine is so severe, she believes she and her son will not survive it. Elijah encourages her not to fear, to go and make a cake for him. He then reassures her that what she has will not run out until it rains. First Kings 17:15 says, "And she went and did as Elijah said. And she and he and her household ate for many days."

Think of it. This widow faced tremendous obstacles. She and her son were facing a drought and did not have very much to sustain themselves. Their future was so bleak that the widow believed they were going to die. If we were in her position, we most likely would have had the same perspective. And yet, even when the outlook is bleak, God sees an even bigger picture, which includes His gracious provision. We can often be so consumed by our circumstances that we miss how God is working in us and around us, what He is actually providing for us, and how we can be eager to participate in what He is doing. Thankfully, this widow believed Elijah that God would provide for her, and she and her son were saved.

God always sees the bigger picture, and His provision is always sufficient. Knowing God and being willing to trust in Him will help us not only to see the bigger picture but to experience it as well. The widow in this story took inventory of her resources—a bit of flour and oil—and she thought they were not enough. But she trusted God with her meager resources and served Him by serving Elijah. She didn't let her circumstance be an excuse; she didn't try to pawn off the responsibility to a neighbor or assume someone else would take care of Elijah. She was invited by God to serve His purpose, and she trusted Him and said yes. As a result, she experienced the extraordinary miracle of God's provision.

Trust is defined as a "firm belief in the reliability, truth, ability, or strength of someone or something." When we encourage you to trust God, we are asking you to firmly believe in the reliability, truth, ability, and strength of Him! Trust God as He leads you in this life, even when your resources seem meager or your circumstances are not desirable. Trust God and be prepared to say yes to Him when He invites you to do His work.

What Do You Have to Work With?

What do you see when you take inventory of what you have in your marriage tool belt? What past experiences is God inviting you to use to fulfill His purposes? What parts of your testimony can you share to point others back to God? What talents might you be able to use to fulfill God's will? What resources do you have that would help you do the ministry work God is inviting you to do? Take inventory of what God has uniquely equipped you with, both individually and as a couple. Write it down so that you can refer back to it again and again. Pray and ask God to reveal them to you so that you don't miss anything. Discuss with your spouse any and all of the tools the two of you have accumulated over your life together. Encourage one another to write down even the things you may think are not good enough to be used by God, the imperfect things, the painful things—all of it. You are a builder, and you need to know what you have to work with.

Once you and your spouse have identified what is in your tool belt, you can prayerfully and humbly submit it to God, knowing confidently that you are already equipped to do the work He has either already invited you to do or will invite you to participate in. After the two of you talk about it and write it down, pray that God will use you. Pray that He will prepare your hearts to say yes to the ministry He has for your marriage.

What Are You Holding Back?

Consider again the story of the widow of Zarephath. She was originally motivated by fear; she wanted to hold back what she had for herself and her son, but had she done so, the results would have been disastrous. Remembering her example, carefully consider if there is anything in your tool belt that you are holding back from God. When the two of you are discussing your inventory, honestly evaluate if there are past relationships or experiences that you refuse to hand over to God. Do you worry that you don't have the financial resources to accomplish anything? Or do you fear embarrassment or rejection? Be transparent in communicating these things with each other, and be sure to give all your fears and insecurities to God.

When we hand it all over to God, especially the things we are afraid to hand over to Him, He doesn't just use us. In God's goodness and grace, He also heals us and transforms us. For example, when we decided to share our marriage struggles online and in our book, we were terrified of what others would think of us. We almost didn't share our story because we were afraid of how people would respond. Yet God invited us to share it with the world, so we submitted to His call and obeyed. As a result, not only did people turn to God and find hope and healing for their marriages, but we too experienced God's healing touch. Being vulnerable with our struggles helped reconcile us to each other and heal those parts of us that used to be a stronghold for the enemy. We may have wrestled with fear in the beginning, but once we started recognizing how God was working in our marriage and in the marriages around us, the more we understood just how much it was worth it to do.

What We See as Inadequate, God Sees as Enough

God sees the bigger picture, the impact of our actions, long before we start to grasp what He is doing. This is why we can trust Him with the tools He has given to us, because He can use even the small things to do big things for His kingdom.

Matthew 14 recounts another extraordinary experience of God's provision, when Jesus miraculously feeds over five thousand people with only five loaves of bread and two fish. Jesus blesses the small amount of food and then His disciples begin to disperse it. Not only is everyone satisfied, but there are also twelve baskets full of leftovers! How in the world does this happen, other than God's faithful and sufficient provision?

In that moment of facing a need to feed the people, the disciples saw only their current circumstances: a lot of people, not enough food to feed them, and not enough money to buy enough food to feed them. Yet because Jesus multiplied the meager resources at hand, the people were fed and satisfied, with an abundance left over. The disciples could only see so far. God sees differently. God sees the bigger picture.

God sees the BIGGER picture.

The disciples, the widow who fed Elijah, and we, too, often regard reality in the flesh, often forgetting to consider God's perspective, but what we see as inadequate, God sees as enough.

Saying Yes to God

The last thing we want you to consider from the story of the widow of Zarephath is that Elijah is a representative of God, sent by God to the widow so that she could feed him. Just like the woman in the story was enduring a physical drought, the world is enduring a spiritual drought. People are turning away from God, fighting against Him, removing mentions of Him, or mocking Him wherever they can. In these times of spiritual drought we are called, like the widow, to use what we have for God's purposes.

Keep this in mind when God sends someone to you to take care of, to feed, to share Scripture with, to share your story with, to generously provide for, even if you are tempted to think that what you have to share is not enough. Remember that what you have been given, God gave to you. Remember that His opinion of what is enough matters and that His provision is sufficient.

Be prepared to say yes to God. Be prepared to respond in obedience. You can trust God as He invites you to use your tool belt to do the work He has already prepared for you and your spouse to do. Consider whether or not God can trust you with what He has given to you. Make it your prayer with your spouse today to confidently say, "Yes, Lord, You can use us. Yes, Lord, You can use that ugly, messy, painful part of our story. Yes, Lord, we will follow You. Yes, Lord, we will obey You. Yes, Lord, what we have is Yours. Yes, Lord, we will trust You."

One couple in particular who have taken inventory of what is in their tool belt and have said yes to God is Isaac and Angie, who became our friends shortly after we moved to the Pacific Northwest. They have eight children and one baby in heaven, lost in a miscarriage. We have witnessed firsthand this couple's faithfulness in living out God's Word. When they endured hardships like the loss of their baby and the collapse of their business, their faith and unity not only remained steadfast, but strengthened. Although they have honestly shared their pain, frustrations, and insecurities, their countenances and words always honored God. They persevered through these trials, reminding each other of the way they should respond, of the example they are setting for their children and others.

Isaac and Angie faithfully use the tools that God has given them to raise godly, respectful children. Their example has impacted our parenting, and we have seen it encourage other parents in our local community as well. In addition to raising their children, they are a hospitable family, inviting us, and many others, into their home to be fed and loved on with conversation and games. In addition, with Angie's extensive experience of childbirth and postpartum, she has made herself available to other women in our fellowship who are in a season of pregnancy and postpartum, offering tips and encouragement for that season of life, something we have truly valued as we have had our children. Finally, Isaac and Angie encourage couples through their blogs and social media (Resoluteman.com and Courageousmom .com).

Isaac and Angie have taken inventory of their tool belt, they consider what can be done with it, and they humbly serve God by using what He has given to them to serve others. The impact they have had in their children's lives, in our lives, in people's lives all around the world because they said yes to God in sharing their experiences, testimony, gifts, and resources—it is all unfathomable. You may not know them yet, but they are impacting this world and the body of Christ simply because they said yes to God and continue to say yes to Him through their obedience.

Take inventory of what is in your marriage tool belt and consider the many ways God might be inviting you and your spouse to work together as a team to use your unique and God-given tools for His glory. Then boldly say, "Yes, Lord! All that You have commanded us, we will do!"

QUESTIONS FOR REFLECTION

1. How do you know you can trust God during the difficult times?
2. How much does God need to accomplish His purposes?
3. Why is it important to take inventory of what is in your marriage tool belt?

Chapter 12

GOD'S WILL FOR
YOUR MARRIAGE

We hope by now you are beginning to see that the One who created the universe and everything in it, the One who invented marriage for the purpose of fulfilling His mission, has uniquely gifted and equipped your marriage to participate in fulfilling His will in this world. You have been challenged and inspired to see your marriage from a heavenly perspective. You have been shown that God, in His infinite and mighty wisdom, designed and purposed the institution of marriage to be an earthly symbol of a divinely beautiful truth. You now see the mystery that has been long hidden up until the time God revealed it to us through His Son, Jesus, and wrote it down by the hands of the apostles, of what the picture of a husband and wife show this lost and dying world. You understand the importance of establishing a biblical foundation from which you will participate in the work of the ministry God invites you to, you have taken inventory of the tools He has

What **MIGHTY WORK** does God have for your marriage to **ACCOMPLISH** in this world?

provided your marriage, and you and your spouse have decided to use it all for God's glory. The only thing that is missing from all of this is the *what*.

What mighty work does God have for your marriage to accomplish in this world?

It's as if the door to the extraordinary life God prepared for you has blown open by the winds of revelation, and the blinding light of what lies ahead is beginning to pour in. It's hard to imagine what good works the Creator of the universe has prepared before the foundations of the earth for you and your spouse to walk in, but that is the very thing this book is encouraging both of you to do.

Maybe you and your spouse are asking yourselves,

- What could God possibly use our marriage for?
- Doesn't God already have enough missionaries, pastors, authors, and youth leaders?
- We're just normal people doing normal things; how can our normal life impact this world for God?
- Doesn't God use special people with special abilities and talents?
- This all sounds really good, but how do we fit in to all of this?

Ministry: Is It Just for Sundays?

Before we get to the *what*, it would be prudent to reveal the source of questions like these. Many of these questions derive from a flawed conception of ministry—of what it is, and where it happens.

Every church we have been a part of has had ministry positions such as executive pastor, youth pastor, senior pastor, and worship pastor. Often these positions are reserved for people with special gifts, training, or a particular degree qualifying them for the task, and they are usually paid. In addition, churches also offer many unpaid positions, places where a person can volunteer, which include directing traffic, being an usher, setting up chairs, or serving coffee. Still others may be more interested in volunteering in the Sunday school, leading a Bible study, serving as an elder or deacon, or serving on a worship team. All of these roles and jobs are good and necessary, especially in a setting where many logistics go into the administration of the church and its worship services. Those who fulfill these responsibilities provide an incredible gift to the body of Christ.

The problem, though, is when we equate "ministry" with these few options, we are left to believe that these are the "only" ministry opportunities we get to choose from. It can also make for a very disconnected and uninspired Monday through Saturday life experience, as if "ministry" is something that happens one day a week and has nothing to do with our daily life. Also, it can become discouraging and deflating when our desire to serve God, our abilities, and our life do not fit into one of these traditional church positions.

Do you think that these specific ministries, the ones mentioned above, were all that God had in mind when He told Adam and Eve to be fruitful and multiply? Do you think this is what Jesus meant when He gave the great commission to His disciples? Do you think these "ministries" are the "good works" that Paul spoke of in Ephesians 2:10 when he says, "For we are his workmanship, created in Christ Jesus for good works, which

God prepared beforehand, that we should walk in them." Please hear our hearts in that we are not putting down any of these specific ministries or the way specific churches have operated. These positions are good and have been impacting the body of Christ year after year. We are simply exposing the lie that these are the *only* ministries available and that unless we have one of these titles, we are not in ministry. The truth is much more powerful.

Ministry is not and never can be boiled down to a handful of specific jobs at your church. Ministry is and always will be what the body of Christ is doing in the world through our lives and actions. A pastor fulfills his part of the ministry with the giftings he has been given in the same way that a stay-at-home mother is doing her part by using all of her gifts, talents, and strength to raise up godly children. You and your marriage are called to the same ministry that the rest of the body is.

We need to stop seeing "ministry" as an isolated event that happens only on Sundays and start seeing it for what it actually is: our everyday existence. If you are in Christ, *you are in ministry*, because Christ is at work in this world through His body. Understanding the truth about what ministry is will help you see, whether big or small, right there in your home or in the public eye, all of the ways God is inviting you to do the work He desires you to do.

Unused Talents

Driving home from the gym one morning, I (Aaron) had the radio tuned to a Christian station. The two hosts that day took a call from a listener who had a deep, smoky, Southern accent.

My immediate thought was *Wow, this guy's voice is powerful!* The hosts noticed as well, commenting on what a perfect radio voice this man had. One host even joked, "Okay, let me hurry up and ask my question before you take my job!"

After the three of them laughed at the notion of this random listener stealing their jobs, the caller humbly said, "Yeah, I know. God gave me a gift, and I pray one day I'll be able to use it."

As I heard his words, my heart sank. All his life this man has had the gift of a strong, striking voice. Why was he still praying that one day he will be able to use it? Is it because he doesn't believe he can use it until someone gives him the opportunity to use it? Is it because he is afraid to use it? Why does the thought of God using his voice for an awesome purpose seem so far from his reality?

This listener is not the only one who has a powerful gift and yet is not using it. Too many of us believe that unless we have been invited by someone in "authority" or have been given an official title, we can't use our gifts. Too many of us are afraid to step out in faith and use what we've been given. I would love for this man to know that right now, God is using his voice and remarks to mirror what others feel about what they have been given. I hope and pray this man, and others who are *in waiting*, will stop relying on someone else to give them permission and find the courage to use their tools today to do something great for God.

Do you remember the parable Jesus told of the master and his servants (Matthew 25)? The master, about to embark on a long journey, entrusts his riches to three of his servants. He gives each of the servants a set amount of talents, or in modern terms, money. To one of the servants the master gives five talents, to another two, to another one—"to each according to his ability" (Matthew 25:15).

The servant who has the most talents entrusted to him goes and invests the money, buying and selling and trading, and his investment proves profitable, effectively doubling his money. The second servant who was given two talents does just as the first servant did and doubles his money as well. The last servant, however, is different. He doesn't do anything with his one talent. Instead of investing it or at least putting it in the bank to earn interest, he buries it.

Of course Jesus is the master in this parable, and we are the servants. Every servant of Christ has been entrusted with some property of the Master, and every servant of Christ is expected to invest His property for the purpose of multiplying it.

This is the long way of saying that you do not need a church position to be in ministry. You do not need permission from your local church to invest what you have been given by God. The very fact that you have been given something means that you have been commissioned.

How many of the three servants in the parable were given talents to steward? All three. How many of the servants used their talents wisely? Only two. Does the third servant have an excuse, since he had only one talent? No! In fact, the master responds to his neglect harshly, calling him wicked and slothful!

Don't be like the servant who hides his talent by burying it. On the contrary, there is a biblical mandate and responsibility as one of the Most High's servants to steward well what He has so graciously entrusted to you, no matter how much or how little that may be.

Your Part in the Body of Christ

Do you think God has people in His body that have no use to Him? Of course not! Everyone plays a part in building up the body of Christ, as Paul notes:

> The body does not consist of one member but of many. If the foot should say, "Because I am not a hand, I do not belong to the body," that would not make it any less a part of the body. And if the ear should say, "Because I am not an eye, I do not belong to the body," that would not make it any less a part of the body. If the whole body were an eye, where would be the sense of hearing? If the whole body were an ear, where would be the sense of smell? But as it is, God arranged the members in the body, each one of them, as he chose. If all were a single member, where would the body be? As it is, there are many parts, yet one body. The eye cannot say to the hand, "I have no need of you," nor again the head to the feet, "I have no need of you" (1 Corinthians 12:14–21).

If you are in Christ, you are a part of His body, and you are not excluded from the ministry that His body is doing in this world.

We cannot tell you exactly *how* you are going to accomplish your role in the body, nor can we tell you the specifics of how your unique experiences, testimonies, talents, and resources will come together in perfect harmony under the control and obedience of the Holy Spirit and His will. We cannot tell you this, because we do not know what God knows. He knows you and your spouse more intimately than even you know each other or yourselves. But what we can tell you without hesitation or fear is *what* the ministry is that you and your marriage have been entrusted with.

This *what* that we so eagerly proclaim to you comes in two parts that must work in perfect tandem. If the two parts are ever separated, both parts not only lose their power but also very quickly work against each other. No, these two things must never be divided.

Serving the Body of Christ

The first part of the *what* is that you must be ready and willing to use everything in your tool belt to bless, serve, and benefit the body of Christ. This will look different for every marriage, but it is the calling of every Christian marriage, and every Christian, for that matter. God has already commissioned you and your spouse to love, serve, and bless other believers with your life and marriage. Philippians 2:4 says it like this, "Let each of you look not only to his own interests, but also to the interests of others."

Much of the New Testament focuses on loving one another. It is this love and unity among believers that will be the greatest message to the world that we are disciples of Jesus (John 13:35), and that God sent Jesus because He loves us (John 17:23).

You must love all your brothers and sisters in Christ. This is your ministry. You must have an earnest desire to protect, heal, love, honor, bless, pray for, engage with, give to, forgive, cry with, laugh with, grow with, and be in complete unity with other members of His body. Christ never intended for the body to be separated and disconnected; rather, His desire is to unite

His body and to expand His kingdom, which leads us to the second part of the ministry God has for your marriage.

Proclaiming the Gospel to the World

The second part of the *what* is that you must use your experiences, testimonies, gifts, and resources to proclaim the gospel to the rest of the world.

When the body of Christ is functioning as it should, unified and building itself up in Christ, the result is a church that preaches the gospel to the lost. As Paul says, "All this is from God, who through Christ reconciled us to himself and gave us the ministry of reconciliation; that is, in Christ God was reconciling the world to himself, not counting their trespasses against them, and entrusting to us the message of reconciliation. Therefore, we are ambassadors for Christ, God making his appeal through us. We implore you on behalf of Christ, be reconciled to God" (2 Corinthians 5:18–20).

The message we have been entrusted with is this: without Christ, we are all dead in our sin and under the wrath of a perfect and just God. We can do nothing in our own strength or merit to earn a right relationship with the Father. However, because the perfectly just God is also perfectly loving, He sent His only begotten Son so that whoever would repent of their wicked ways and believe Jesus died and was resurrected would be reconciled to the Father.

When we say yes to living like Jesus and forsake our old way of life, our once broken and unredeemed nature is now fully and completely made right before God. Because of Jesus Christ, and His sacrifice on the cross, we are now able to have a right relationship with the One who created us. And now we, the reconciled, become the reconcilers. The body of Christ, with all its parts, has this one mission and one call to share the message of salvation in Jesus Christ, the forgiveness of sin, the new creation through rebirth in the Holy Spirit, and most importantly, the right standing before God.

What a beautiful ministry. What a worthy call. Not only have you been saved and transformed, but you also have been invited to participate in the work that Jesus came to do. This has been God's will for you and your marriage from the very beginning. As Peter so beautifully states, "Once you were not a people, but now you are God's people; once you had not received mercy, but now you have received mercy" (1 Peter 2:10). As the people of God and as children of the Creator, it is our inheritance to take on the family business of proclaiming with our words, actions, and love for one another that Christ came to reconcile the world to God.

This is the truth that animates everything we do. This is our full-time spiritual vocation, and it pleases God when we do it with everything we have been given. Everything we do, plan, create, and pursue is motivated by a desire to fulfill this will of the Father of sharing His good news.

No matter what ministry work you and your spouse choose to do, whether you fill a position in your church or pursue something completely different, the message is the same. It is *His* message. You and your spouse have no reason to stress or worry over the details of how you will share God's message. All you need to do is humbly submit your marriage to God and pray, asking Him to reveal the details to you. Be willing to say yes to Him as He guides you to what He created your marriage to do.

QUESTIONS FOR REFLECTION

1. Do you assume that "ministry" happens only Sundays? How might that belief limit your effectiveness in building God's kingdom?
2. Have you been waiting for permission to use your tool belt for ministry?
3. How do you and your spouse serve the body of Christ?
4. How do you proclaim the gospel to the world?

Chapter 13

DREAMING TOGETHER

On January 6, 2017 we celebrated our ten-year wedding anniversary with a romantic four-course dinner at a restaurant in town. The restaurant itself wasn't that fancy, being an old Craftsman-style home converted to a quaint little eatery. The wood floors creaked under the steps of the servers, and a cold draft from some unknown source made us shiver. However, the flavor of our meal was fancy, the way the chef plated our meal was fancy, and the price for our dinner was definitely fancy. The ambiance inside the restaurant was quiet and candlelit, a blessed treat for us parents of littles.

The first hour of our date we talked about our ten years of marriage, reminiscing over the memories we have made together. That conversation led us into dreaming about the coming year, sharing ideas that had been on our hearts and wondering what God might be inviting us to do next.

My wife reminded me of our dream to host a weekend marriage retreat. As we began to consider this endeavor, we talked about the purpose. We didn't want to do a typical marriage retreat, focused on problem solving or resting and reconnecting. Rather, we decided we wanted to inspire couples to chase after the extraordinary purpose God has for their marriage. The more we talked about this dream, the more our excitement grew.

Although we had a handful of what-ifs, fears, and insecurities, by the end of our date we were determined to say yes to God in faith that He was inviting us to do this. We spent the next few weeks counting the cost and figuring out logistical details. Once the details were in place, we created a website for couples to register. We called it the Marriage After God Gathering and opened registration for the event on Valentine's Day, hoping couples would join us but also fearing that no one would sign up! We were shocked by how quickly we were notified of couples signing up, and we were thrilled when the gathering quickly reached capacity.

Although we had never hosted an event of this magnitude, we realized that God had equipped us with the tools we needed to handle it successfully. God had stirred up a dream in our hearts to host this event, and it became a reality, because we were willing to say yes. The impact of our yes was revealed to us as soon as the event began. The interactions with the couples, the discussions on building a biblical foundation, the sharing of our concept of the tool belt, and the encouragement to these couples to dream together made for an inspiring time. We witnessed the impact of this message on those couples, and we knew we had to find a way to spread this message even farther. That is when God began stirring a new dream in our hearts, to use the content we shared from the Marriage After God Gathering and present it in a book that could find its way to you!

The Next Step in Your Marriage Journey

Dreaming together as a couple has been an incredible experience. We both recognize the value in sharing our hearts with one another, being vulnerable, and sharing how God might be working in us and in our marriage. We believe important things bubble up to the surface when a husband and wife purpose to dream together. Talking and dreaming together is an opportunity to intimately communicate and connect. So the next step in your marriage journey is to dream together about how God might be inviting you to work as a team to fulfill His purposes.

At the beginning of every year since we said "I do," we have set time aside to dream together about the upcoming year. We consider what is already on our plates and discuss goals God might want us to pursue. We take time to reevaluate what is in our tool belt and how it can be used to glorify God. We consider any new financial opportunities to use our money to bless the body of Christ. We share any book ideas or projects that might be stirring in our hearts. We talk about the condition of our relationships and how we can make them better, including our relationship with each other and with our children. We examine our parenting and strategize ways to improve, and we analyze any other opportunities that God may be putting in our path. After we discuss what we have and the direction we should go, we submit it all to the Lord with open hands, asking Him to continue to lead us. We often recall Proverbs 16:3: "Commit your work to the LORD, and your plans will be established."

Although we are intentional about goal setting at the beginning of every year, dreaming together does not just happen once a year. In fact, we take time every few months and sometimes

DREAMING together is an exercise that is **IMPORTANT** for every marriage.

weekly to bring up new dreams or talk about the progress we are making with current goals. Continually considering our roles in the purpose and plans God has for our marriage has been a driving motivation for us as we dream together.

This time that we spend dreaming together is a unifying experience. Communicating our current circumstances, progress, and desires to each other is an intimate experience as we expose what is going on inside our hearts. It also helps us get on the same page as we look forward to the coming year and what our parts will be in the grand scheme of God's endeavors.

Dreaming together is an exercise that is important for every marriage after God to participate in. Setting goals and casting a vision for the future strengthens the bond between a husband and wife, stirring up hope for what may come. We have discovered that having hope for the future helps produce perseverance in the day-to-day movement of life. Knowing what it is that we are working toward and working for gives purpose to all the decisions we make today.

The same is true for your marriage. Dreaming together gets your hearts and minds aligned as you and your spouse honestly discuss important matters like the condition of your marriage and what can be improved upon. Dreaming together is also exciting as you and your spouse agree to pursue specific desires God has planted in your hearts. Dreaming together and goal setting is a team-building practice that cultivates oneness in marriage.

How to Dream Together

There are a few things to consider before you and your spouse start dreaming together. These are things that will benefit your marriage as you devote time to thinking about how God will use your marriage in the coming years.

The first thing is that your dreaming must be established on a biblical foundation and biblical priorities. A dream to pursue ministry or a new business or a personal endeavor must never take precedence over caring for your marriage or your family.

Remember that you and your spouse are one, so you must dream *together*. Oneness is vital in the ministry you do through your marriage. It can be so easy to dream alone or to believe that your own dream is of utmost value. Take time to consider the details of your dreams or the ideas you believe God might be leading you to pursue, and then talk about them with your spouse. Be sure the two of you are on the same page and in agreement before you move forward.

Another important part of dreaming together is listening to each other. It would not be beneficial for you and your spouse to come to the table eager to share your hearts with one another, but rather than listening intently, you just wait for your chance to speak. The Bible tells us clearly to be "quick to hear, slow to speak" (James 1:19). Be sure you truly listen to your spouse. Hear what they have to say and respond to their words before moving the conversation in a different direction. Listen when your spouse gives you feedback on a dream or goal you present, and do not get defensive or frustrated if your spouse is not in agreement with pursuing that dream or goal. Instead, submit your goal to God in prayer and ask Him to reveal His will about it.

When you dream together about future projects, types of work, or events, the focus should not be on what you want, but rather on what God wants to do through your marriage to build His kingdom. This means that you are sensitive to where God is leading you and your spouse. This also means that you may have a dream in your heart or your spouse might have a desire that isn't ready to be pursued just yet. Ask God how you and your spouse can join in where God is already working and believe that His timing is best.

A marriage after God is one where the husband and wife walk with humble hearts before the Lord and with each other. Marriage is not about you and what you want; neither is it all about your spouse. Instead, yield your hearts to the Lord and acknowledge that your marriage has a far greater purpose than being the means by which you are fulfilled. Your marriage is the means by which *God's* purposes are fulfilled and He is glorified. For it is not your message you are striving to spread, it is not your mission you are pursuing, and it is not your kingdom you are building. Everything you and your spouse do is for God's message, God's mission, and the building up of God's kingdom. And as you chase after God, you will discover that your personal dreams and desires begin to align with His.

The last two things to consider when it comes to dreaming together is that you should make this time with your spouse a sacred time by being completely present and you should come prepared.

When you and your spouse dream together, make sure you protect that time from distractions. If you have children, hire a babysitter or spend time after the kids have gone to bed or early in the morning before they wake up, so you can create space for the two of you to really focus your hearts and your attention on each other. Be sure to stay off of your phones and avoid the distractions of dinging notifications. This is a time for the two of you to openly talk about your heart's desire for things to come. Be fully present.

When you do come together to dream about the future and what God might be asking you and your spouse to do, come prepared. I (Jennifer) love to take along a few sheets of paper and a pen to take notes. You can also use a whiteboard, a laptop, or a notes app on your phone. A great idea would be to invest in a blank lined journal that can be used to record your dreams. If you write it all down, you will have something concrete to refer back to as the two of you work toward specific goals.

You can also come prepared mentally by thinking ahead of time about what ideas, or areas of life, you want to chat about. Is there something urgent and pressing? Has it been a while since you talked about your children? Is there a major transition you need to discuss, like moving or a job change? Giving some thought to the things you want to discuss will help you clearly navigate the conversation with the set time that you have together. Plan ahead by being prepared.

Do you need more ideas of what you can discuss? We've provided a list of sample questions at the end of the book, but for now, here's a brief list of categories you can consider communicating about: the condition of your marriage, pressing personal needs, parenting issues, job or career choices, finances, your community, where you feel God leading you, what God might be asking you to do, and potential projects you could do together.

This is also a great time to evaluate the progress the two of you are making on current goals. During this time together consider all of the vital elements we have already covered in this book, taking time to discuss each one. Evaluate your marriage in light of the seven marks of a marriage after God. Are there marks you two can be working on in your relationship? Are there marks already evident in your marriage that you can acknowledge and celebrate? What about your marital foundation—are the two of you in God's Word? Are you good stewards with finances? Are you participating in fellowship with other believers? These are significant areas of marriage that we don't want you to overlook or skip over. Ask each other questions about where your marriage is at and where God wants it to be. Truly listen as you transparently share these details with each other.

This is a great time to take inventory of what is in your marriage tool belt! Honestly discuss all of the experiences, testimonies, gifts, and resources that fill your tool belt. Dream out loud about the different ways God could use your tools to impact His kingdom. This is not a one-time event; it is now a way of doing life together. Revisit and evaluate your tool belt often!

You might also ask each other questions about the future. Where do you want to be in five, ten, or twenty-five years? What vision do you have for the future? What priorities do you want to put your effort toward? What are things you absolutely want to start tackling today? As your list of goals becomes clearer, make a plan that the two of you can agree on to work toward accomplishing those goals. What will you commit to doing in order to achieve these goals? What might you have to give up in order to get it done? Casting a vision together for the future of your marriage is an intimate experience where hope for the future stimulates perseverance for today.

Strategize—and Pray

Now that the two of you have been challenged and inspired to make sure your marriage has a strong biblical foundation, you have taken inventory of what is in your tool belt, and you have made it a priority to set goals, it is time for the nitty-gritty of creating a strategy that will help the two of you accomplish the work God has prepared for you to do. Having a well-thought-out strategy is essential because you can clarify who is responsible for what as you pursue the work of the ministry as a team. In sports there are specific requirements and expectations for each team player. Marriage is similar in that a husband and wife are both team players who should be eager to help the team as a whole advance toward winning or accomplishing the goal. In order for this to actually happen, we must know our responsibilities.

In our marriage, as we focus on specific goals throughout the week, we have a strategy that seems to work well for both of us. We break down what needs to be accomplished each day in order to successfully reach our goals. We use a 3 x 5 card to list the things we each need to do to fulfill our part, and we hang on to that card until we get it done. This has helped us to make reaching our goals a reality. Another strategy we utilize is sending either an email or a text message with a list of goals or appointments we have to prioritize for the week. This helps us be on the same page as we work together. Since your goals and your dreams will look different from ours, your strategies may be different. Take time to examine and create strategies that will best fit your marriage and the work you and your spouse have to accomplish.

Lastly, as the two of you have fun talking about your dreams, goals, and strategies, take a moment to pray together, submitting all of it to God. Thank Him for where He has brought you, the gift of the tool belt that He has given you, the dreams He has planted in your hearts, and the work you will do as a team. Ask

God to lead you as you use what He has given to you for His glory. Also, ask God to open your eyes to the many opportunities He is inviting you to participate in as you use your tools to bless each other and others. Pray for your marriage, pray for each other, pray for your children, pray for your community. Never cease to pray, for this is God's will for you (1 Thessalonians 5:16–18)!

The connection you create with your spouse when you dream and pray together is powerful. Dreaming and praying together shows your spouse how much you are invested in your marriage and how much you desire God to be at the center of it all. It is choices like these that actively affirm love in marriage. It cultivates closeness and it produces good fruit. Make dreaming together an experience you love to do and decide to do it often. Try it today!

QUESTIONS FOR REFLECTION

1. Why is it important to dream together?
2. Pick one or two topics from the list on pages 234–238 and spend time dreaming together.

Part 5

YOUR MARRIAGE FOR
GOD'S PURPOSES:
THE IMPACT

Chapter 14

ORDINARY PEOPLE
WITH EXTRAORDINARY
MARRIAGES

When I proposed to Jennifer, I promised three things: that I would love her to the best of my ability, that I would trust God as He leads us, and that I would pray for an extraordinary life with her by my side. Through the dating and engaged season of our relationship, we would pray for our future marriage, and we asked God to use us to do great things for His sake. We prayed for an extraordinary marriage. Although we didn't know the specific opportunities God would give us as husband and wife, we believed an extraordinary marriage was possible and we desired it.

A few years into our marriage, when we were going through hardships and tempted to divorce, I would lie in bed at night and pray over our marriage. I felt prompted to remain committed to the promise I submitted to God at the beginning of our relationship, asking Him for an extraordinary marriage. We asked God to do the extraordinary in us and through us. The hope of having an extraordinary marriage kept a flicker of light burning amidst the darkness, helping us navigate those next steps we took.

Now, after more than a decade of marriage, we can clearly see how God took an ordinary man and woman, binding us together through marriage, and led us to experience an extraordinary life together. Every day we get to participate in the amazing work God has trusted us to carry out. God has been faithful to answer our prayer, and still, we continue to pray for the extraordinary opportunities He has for us in the future.

In addition to our continued commitment to prayer for God to use our marriage for His glory, we pray that you and your spouse will also live out an extraordinary marriage as you faithfully pursue the purposes God has for your marriage.

Extraordinary is defined as "very unusual or remarkable, amazing, sensational." Having an extraordinary marriage means that your relationship with your spouse looks different than everyone else's. You stand out in the world, because you don't operate according to the world's standards or pressures. Your marriage is amazing and remarkable, the things you and your spouse do and the purposes you pursue together are incredible, unbelievable, world changing. Extraordinary is not measured by whether you are famous or wealthy or have lots of followers on social media. It is not measured by who you know or even where you have been. Extraordinary is much more than all of this.

You and your spouse may be ordinary people, but your marriage is extraordinary as you practice righteousness, walk in the Spirit, and reflect the love story of Christ and the church.

You and your spouse may be **ORDINARY** people, but your marriage is **EXTRAORDINARY.**

Experiencing the extraordinary opportunities God has for you and your spouse is a byproduct and fruit of walking faithfully with God.

The extraordinary things that ordinary people do for God reveal the heart of God. He is the One that puts those desires in the hearts of His people. His followers who boldly chase after His will do not work for praise or merit; rather, they work to please God, motivated by a passion to serve Him and build His kingdom.

The Power of Story

We have had a chance to tell our story. Our hope is always to use what we have experienced to direct people's hearts closer to God's heart. We believe personal stories and testimonies are powerful because they have the ability to reach down deeply and move people in ways that nothing else can. Stories often reveal things from a unique perspective that perhaps would not be seen any other way. We believe God uses stories and testimonies of His work in the world to show people His power, grace, and unconditional love. Exposing how God is at work in the world reminds us of who God is and what can be done when we say yes to Him.

Over the years we have been blessed to see examples of God at work in many different marriages. If we hadn't seen these examples, we may not have known what it could look like for God to work in ours. So we'd like to share with you just a handful of stories of ordinary couples experiencing an extraordinary life and marriage because they boldly chase a marriage after God. The work that these couples have been able to accomplish has built up the kingdom of God. These stories have touched our hearts, and we are certain they will touch yours as well.

We want you to consider the journey these couples have been on and how God used their marriage tool belt for His extraordinary purposes. The ministry work these couples have pursued came from the heart of God, delivered to them as a purpose to fulfill, a purpose that united them as husband and wife, as they committed themselves to the Lord's work. They were willing to say yes, to persevere and rely on God, even when hardships and trials came their way, and they continue to walk faithfully to this day. The unique impact of each one of these marriages is extraordinary.

We hope these real-life stories inspire you to consider the power of God and the richness of His love for you and your spouse. May these stories open your eyes to all the people His gospel will reach because you, too, have chosen to faithfully walk in His ways.

A Special Kind of Adoption

Down South, in an average old home, at the end of a quiet cul-de-sac, lives a beautiful family. Basketfuls of shoes ranging in different sizes sit by the front door; the island in the kitchen is covered with daily essentials like fruit, medicine, homework, and hospital paperwork begging for attention; and the dining room wall is filled with the portraits of nine precious smiling children.

Art and Jen have a very full house, but that wasn't always the case. When they married, Jen became the stepmother of Art's son from a previous marriage. They had two children together, a girl and then a boy. But then, after they struggled with infertility and the loss of a baby, their neighbor invited them to church. Over the course of a few months, God opened their eyes to the sin that separated them from the Lord. For the first time in their lives, both Art and Jen believed that Jesus died on the cross for their sins and was resurrected three days later in victory over death, making a way for them to spend eternity with God. They were forever changed by His amazing grace.

Art and Jen began building the foundation of their family based on the Word of God. They read the Bible to their children and prayed with them, teaching them what they were learning about what it means to have faith in God. They submitted their hearts to God and desired to walk in obedience to what His Word commanded. The fruit of the Spirit, the definition of love, the example of Christ, and everything else they encountered in the Bible changed how they treated each other in marriage and how they responded to daily circumstances. That doesn't mean they didn't experience hardship, but when trials came, they increased their dependence on God, refining and strengthening their faith.

As Art and Jen chased after God's will for their marriage and family, a desire to adopt rose up in their hearts. Over the period of five short years, Art and Jen adopted not one, but six special needs children from China. They have had a very busy and full house as they work together to tend to the needs of their beautiful children. Each one of their child's adoption stories, how God brought these children into their home and provided the funds necessary to do so, are incredible testimonies that bring glory to God. Each one of these children has special needs, requiring Art and Jen to arrange their schedule and finances in a way that supports these needs, whether it is a weekly counseling session, a new pair of glasses, or another trip to the hospital for corrective surgery. Art and Jen have faithfully said yes to God for all of it because they have witnessed God's faithfulness and have been forever changed by it.

They have battled with fears, insecurities, doubt, and weaknesses, but they attest to the power of the Holy Spirit correcting them, comforting them, and directing them along the way. Many times they have been side by side, face down on the bedroom floor, in prayer and in tears. Yet, no matter the hardships they encounter, they continue to trust God. Their faithfulness is evident in their hearts and on their faces. As they told us, "When we focus on eternity and the many people who have yet to make decisions to trust and follow Jesus, those challenges fall to the side. The Lord has quickened our hearts and helped us to have an urgency for the lost. We have no time to waste."

Art and Jen might have their hands and hearts full of family responsibilities, but they are also full-time missionaries working on staff with Family Life, an organization that is reaching millions of marriages and families around the world to bring them the gospel.

We asked Art and Jen how the Lord has revealed Himself to them, and this was their response: "Holy ground. We have experienced it in orphanages in China surrounded by rows of silent babies. We have experienced it in hospital waiting rooms with big questions. We once tore up divorce papers with a couple in their living room as we watched a husband give his life to Jesus. Holy ground. We would have never imagined in a million years we would be living where we are living, working where we are working, and absolutely never imagined adopting or having this many children. There are many heartaches and trials we never imagined as well. We have learned it is all His grace. He will direct our steps. We have learned that where He calls, He provides. We wish we had learned earlier that obedience is worth far more than the temporary satisfaction we crave instead. We have learned that His plans and His love for us are far greater than we could ever imagine. He is faithful. He is worthy."

If you were to ask Art and Jen what unique tools they may have been given to do all that they have done and continue to pursue, Jen would say in the sweetest Southern accent, "Oh, we're not fancy people, we just love the Lord." They would tell you they are just ordinary people, convinced that God loves them deeply, and that He loves you too!

Love Thy Neighbor

As they headed up the stairs to their apartment for the first time after their honeymoon, Ben and Catherine were quick to say yes to an opportunity sent from God. They ran into Chris, a new neighbor. They spent a little time introducing each other, and at the end of their conversation, Ben and Catherine offered their new neighbor some bread they had just picked up at the bakery. This connection with Chris didn't end there. In fact, they continued to build their relationship with him, making small talk when they passed in the shared parking lot, inviting him over for breakfast and home projects, and hosting him and his parents for a home-cooked meal. Although they have all since moved away, theirs is a friendship that continues to this day.

Ben and Catherine are faithful friends of ours and faithful stewards of what God has given to them. They encourage one another to remain obedient to the Word of God, faithfully living out His command to "love your neighbor" (Mark 12:31). Their thoughtfulness in serving and loving others has become a defining mark of their marriage. People know them by their ministry and gift of hospitality. Their marriage has been used time and time again to welcome, comfort, provide, and sustain their neighbors, family, and friends. They are an ordinary couple who choose to be the hands and feet of Jesus, experiencing extraordinary encounters with the people God has placed in their lives.

They would not hesitate to tell you the amazing ways God uses food to spark a relationship with neighbors. They walk their children around the block offering cookies to neighbors for no reason other than they happened to be baking that day. They have sit-down dinners with their next-door neighbors; they attend their neighbor's son's soccer games to show their support of the whole family; they invite neighbors to share their opinions about backyard projects; and they ask older neighbors for advice, calling on them to glean from their wisdom. These are all opportunities Ben and Catherine have said yes to, for the purpose of sharing their lives with others. They share the gift of the gospel through the example of how they live, through the gift of connection, and through the power of communication.

Ben and Catherine have recognized a need for connection in our world. They have committed to being present in people's lives, saying, "It's underestimated in our hurried culture today, but people stopping, sitting, sharing over a meal is healthy and powerful. Often times it's not even a meal, but something even simpler, like a cup of coffee."

Ben and Catherine have touched the hearts of many people through their willingness to serve side by side in their marriage.

Their hearts are in agreement as they carry out God's calling for their marriage, and they want to encourage you with these words: "Jesus told us that it doesn't take much—faith the size of a mustard seed—to move mountains, and sometimes all it takes is a simple knock on a door with some cookies or an open invitation for conversation, and there you go, trust is built and a relationship can begin to develop. Simple. It has been an absolute pleasure to see how God continues to use us, better together than apart, to be a center of hospitality and an open home to those around us."

When we asked Ben and Catherine what challenges they have had to overcome to say yes to God in the ministry opportunities of hospitality, loving their neighbors, or opening up their home, they shared a beautiful perspective about boundaries, saying, "Having kids and making sure they feel treasured and prioritized by us can be a challenge. Sometimes saying 'no' to a church dinner or declining a conversation with a neighbor is the best decision, so that we can prioritize an overdue night of hanging out with our kids. Our ministry to our children comes first; they are our blessing from the Lord."

The Power of a Painful Past

Sean and Katie were high school sweethearts, marrying each other at just twenty-two years old. They are the first to admit they were immature when they got married and didn't fully understand the complexity of their union until years later when they began pursuing God's plan for their marriage.

As a preteen, Katie was obsessed with controlling her weight and struggled with many different forms of eating disorders. For nearly a decade she experienced the vicious cycles of bingeing, purging, dieting, and excessive exercise in an attempt to control her weight, which fluctuated from low to high to everything in between.

The constant stress Katie was putting on her body left her extremely fatigued and anxious. When she was in college she realized she didn't want to live that way anymore. She didn't want to be a slave to the need to control what she ate and how much she exercised. So she called on God to help her win this dark battle she had been wrestling with. God was faithful to help Katie live a healthier, more balanced life, and Sean was by her side, encouraging her along the way. Instead of fighting for control over her weight, she gave God control over it, trusting Him to lead her. Eventually, Katie's heart and mind were transformed, and she slowly changed the way she viewed her beauty, her weight, and her relationship with God. Although this transformation didn't happen overnight, the more she sought after God, the freer she felt.

Katie went on to graduate and became a registered nurse. She was passionate about learning as much as she could about the human body and developed a vision for living a well-balanced life.

Meanwhile, Sean was busy with four franchises of Dippin' Dots, which he opened at age nineteen. Unfortunately, Sean had to close these stores due to employee incompetence. When new business opportunities arose, Sean struggled with the fear of failure, worrying that he didn't have what it took to run a business.

Katie's painful past of struggling to control her weight and her experience with eating disorders was part of her story that she could have buried. She could have chosen to walk in her new freedom and never look back at her past experiences or ever talk about them again. Sean could have been hindered from starting a new business because of his fear of failing. Both of them could have said no to the opportunity God invited them to pursue, and they would have missed an extraordinary experience of using their marriage tool belt for His glory. But that is not how this story ends.

Katie was motivated by her painful past to understand how to live a healthy, well-balanced life. She was willing to share her story to bring glory to God in hopes of encouraging others to give their hearts to Him. Sean was supportive in helping turn Katie's journey with food and exercise into a business that would utilize both of their passions and skills to bring glory to God.

So Katie and Sean founded Dashing Dish, an incredible website that shares Katie's story in addition to many more resources that encourage healthy living. Not only has Sean been a supportive husband in this endeavor, but he also directed the creative design and function for this beautiful site that has encouraged millions of people.

Katie and Sean were willing to say yes to God. They dug into their tool belt, and they didn't hold anything back from God. He let them use all of it, and because of their obedience, their impact in this world continues to be extraordinary.

When we asked Sean and Katie how God has shown Himself to them, they replied, "We have both learned through obedience, and we continue to learn that being in the center of His will is the best and safest place to be!"

The Way God Moves

Cecilia had experience as a dancer, choreographer, and dance instructor. Her husband, Nathan, had years of experience starting and running businesses, including a non-profit. God planted a vision in Cecilia's heart to produce a dance show where the proceeds would go to support a family whose child was battling cancer. So together they launched The Movement Project.

When Nathan and Cecilia hosted their first dance show, they didn't foresee that God had much bigger plans for it. What was going to be a one-time event, God turned into a non-profit. They now host an annual dance show that raises money for other families with children going through cancer.

Nathan and Cecilia recognized the way God was moving and inviting them, as a team, to work together to do something great for their community. Cecilia knew and understood what it would take to produce a great show, but turning it into a non-profit required the skills and experience her husband had already accumulated through the years. Their unity and their willingness to say yes to God's bigger picture have created an incredible event where others can use their gifts of dance and administration to support the needs of their community. Now their contribution of time, energy, and hard work continues to impact their community year after year.

When Nathan and Cecilia first married, they decided what they wanted their marriage and family to be about. They saw themselves as a husband and wife duo, a family who would pursue joyful opportunities together. They were confident their marriage had purpose, but they didn't see it as a ministry. When God led them on this journey of creating The Movement Project, they each wrestled with doubt, wondering if seats would be filled or money would be raised. Despite their doubt, they had confidence God was moving in them, and they trusted Him with every detail.

When we asked Nathan and Cecilia how they pursue this ministry together, they shared, "We made a commitment that we can't let The Movement Project steal the joy in our marriage and in our home. For us, that means paying close attention to how we are feeling while planning, preparing, and growing the organization. If at any point we are feeling robbed of this joy, we both remind each other what we are doing and why we are doing it. And if we need to take a break and stop, we do."

We also invited this couple to share a handful of tips they might have to encourage other couples based on their experience of working in ministry together. Cecilia said, "The process of sharing one another's vision is vital and uplifting. Knowing the dreams God has put on your spouse's heart is encouraging. Lean on one another when things are hard. Rely on your spouse's expertise—don't try to diminish their God-given abilities because of your own pride." Nathan added, "Encourage, encourage, encourage your spouse throughout the process. Let your spouse know you see the awesome work they are doing. Also, just listen when your spouse needs you to listen and follow through with things they ask you to do. Remember, it is not about you."

Marriage as Ministry

There are many more stories of ordinary people doing extraordinary things for God that we could highlight if we had room in this book to fit them all in. We are inspired by the faith in God's people to say yes to the opportunities that are scary, challenging, or don't always make sense. These are all God's stories, testimonies that reveal His heart for mankind.

These people and many others have submitted their hearts to God and have given Him permission to do the extraordinary in their lives. They are ordinary people doing extraordinary things. These are people just like you.

We hope some of these stories will encourage you and show you how extraordinary to God may look different from how the world would define it. Understanding what "extraordinary" is and desiring God to move mightily in your marriage will help you and your spouse spot how He may want to use you now and in the future. No matter where you are in your journey, know that you can trust God to guide you, and never stop praying for His extraordinary will to be done.

When we invited each of these couples to share their stories, the first question we asked all of them was: When you got married, did you see your marriage as a ministry?

All of them replied, "No!" And to be honest, when we got married, we didn't see our marriage as a ministry either. But what we have discovered, and what they have discovered as well, is that as a husband and wife submit to God's ways, it becomes evident that marriage is, indeed, a ministry.

As we embrace the perspective of marriage being a ministry, we become more confident in the ways God moves through us. The extraordinary takes place. God's will is fulfilled. And then our stories and testimonies of God's unconditional love get shared with others, becoming a spark, a catalyst to inspire other husbands and wives to see their marriage as a ministry, to embrace the journey God has for them, and to fulfill the good works He prepared for them to do as a team, for His glory.

QUESTIONS FOR REFLECTION

1. Do you see your marriage as a ministry? If not, how might having that perspective change your marriage? If so, how has God ministered to others through your marriage?
2. Which couple in this chapter most inspired you? Or think of a couple who inspires you. How might their example be a catalyst for you to discover and develop your own ministry as a couple?

Chapter 15

STRONGER TOGETHER

At twenty-one years old and with very little life experience, I (Aaron) had no idea what marriage would be like with my future wife. My lack of foresight and naiveté about marriage made it all the easier to ask Jennifer to be my wife. I couldn't have known the hard journey we were about to embark on. I couldn't have imagined the impact we would one day have on the world through our marriage. However, I did know that God would bind us together, and I was confident that whatever we did and wherever we went, it was going to be together, with God and for God.

When I proposed to Jennifer, our hearts were aligned with this vision of chasing after God together. That day I gave her a ring engraved with the words of Ecclesiastes 4:12 (NIV): "A cord of three strands is not quickly broken." This verse is a portion of a longer passage that reminds us of the powerful benefit of companionship: "Two are better than one, because they have a good reward for their toil. For if they fall, one will lift up his fellow. But woe to him who is alone when he falls and has not another

Your marriage is a **GIFT**—not just to the two of you, but to this **WORLD.**

to lift him up! Again, if two lie together, they keep warm, but how can one keep warm alone? And though a man might prevail against one who is alone, two will withstand him—a threefold cord is not quickly broken" (Ecclesiastes 4:9–12).

There is power and safety when you and your spouse stand together. But there is infinitely more power when you and your spouse are bound together with God, because a threefold cord is not quickly broken. A marriage after God is a powerful tool in the hands of the almighty God.

Your marriage is a gift—not just to the two of you, but to this world. The impact your unity in marriage can have is unfathomable. You can fight against each other, going in different directions, which will hinder or destroy what God might want to do through your marriage; or you can choose to hold each other's hands and persevere, running in the same direction, with the same vision, fused together and bound by God, confident of the purpose and power of your marriage.

God designed you and your spouse to be ambassadors of holy love to a hurting world. Rather than the inwardly focused perspective defining so many love stories commonly expressed as "you and me against the world," God desires you to embrace the rich and meaningful mission of "you and me *for* the world." Consider the impact that your love for each other and your love for God could make on the rest of the world. Your love story, your unique marriage, has a great purpose to serve.

A marriage after God seeks God every single day, with persistence and passion, eager to serve Him as a team for His kingdom purposes, to be a light in this world and a reflection of Christ's love for His church. A husband and wife chasing after God know every aspect of their marriage is for proclaiming the gospel of Jesus

Christ; they are not ashamed to share about it, and they are confident in the impact they are making in the world around them.

You and your spouse can have a marriage after God. You can use your marriage to build the kingdom of God and spread the gospel. It requires knowing God and believing in His ability to lead you and provide for your lives and your marriage. Proverbs 3:5–6 says, "Trust in the LORD with all your heart, and do not lean on your own understanding. In all your ways acknowledge him, and he will make straight your paths."

To acknowledge God does not simply mean to give a head nod like you would as you pass by a friend at church. That type of acknowledgment is meaningless as you recognize His presence, yet continue on in your own ways. Rather, *acknowledge* means that you know God's ways, that He is the ultimate authority in your life, and that you submit to His leadership. Having a reverent and humble heart that is yielded to God in this way cultivates intimacy in your relationship with Him as you learn who God is and how He leads. Intimacy with God is knowing Him and being known by Him. Take a moment to think about the impact you and your spouse can make as you see your marriage in light of knowing God and being fully known by Him.

No matter what God calls you to do, no matter where He calls you to live, no matter who He brings into your family, no matter what your circumstances, your goal is to work together as one for the kingdom of God. You and your spouse are one. You are a team. Work together by communicating respectfully, seek to understand each other, and encourage growth in each other on a daily basis. As you practice working together as a team in the day-to-day responsibilities, it will benefit you as you pursue additional dreams God plants in your hearts in the future.

A marriage after God **SEEKS** God every single day, with **PERSISTENCE** and passion.

There are two things that have helped us to work together as a team. Whether it has been working on our marriage, our parenting, our business, or other projects we have set out to accomplish together, the two things that have unified us as a couple are first, being effective communicators, and second, having fun along the way.

Communicate Effectively

Communication is key for every marriage, and yours is no exception. Be people who communicate maturely, clearly, humbly, and respectfully. Communication is a gift from God and a tool that will help you navigate every circumstance you face in life.

The story of the tower of Babel reminds us of the power of communication. In Genesis 11:6 God says, "Behold, they are one people, and they have all one language, and this is only the beginning of what they will do. And nothing that they propose to do will now be impossible for them."

Think about what that means and how it relates to your marriage. Those building the tower were unified and spoke only one language, and God acknowledged that nothing would be impossible for them. Now imagine what you and your spouse could accomplish if you are unified and effective communicators. If there is power in effective communication, this means that the enemy is sure to attack this area of your marriage. So defend your marriage from the attacks of the enemy by being intentional in the way you communicate. Don't be discouraged when arguments come up or something is said that was not fruitful. You and your spouse are practicing how to communicate every day. Part of communication is also listening, so practice how to be good listeners. Being effective communicators will make you stronger together as you work in unity to further God's kingdom purposes.

Have Fun along the Way

Having fun along the way is also extremely important. Your marriage was meant for you and your spouse to enjoy. Don't get too caught up in the mundane routine of life, or be too serious with each other, or stress out as you try to control everything, all the while missing out on the joy of the journey. God gives you and your spouse many ways each day to enjoy each other's company, and it is up to you to take advantage of those moments. Find ways to have fun together, laugh, and play more. Kiss each other randomly and let each other know that although the work you pursue is important, nothing will ever be more important than the love you have for each other. By doing this, you will strengthen your bond of unity, while building up security and trust in your spouse's heart. Choose to engage with your spouse in ways that will make you stronger together.

Aaron and I like to have fun in our marriage by scheduling a weekly date night. That is when we spend quality time together, doing an activity, trying new food, or simply enjoying our favorite foods at our favorite restaurant. We like to have fun by being physical with each other. When we are on a walk or a hike with the kids we will hold hands, or I will wrap my arm around Aaron's back as we walk side by side. We have fun in the car by turning the music up loud and dancing silly. We have fun just driving in the car together. We don't even need a destination; we just enjoy the fresh air and company. We enjoy exploring antique shops. We have fun going to the movies and we have fun staying up late, chatting. These are just a handful of ways we enjoy each other's company.

In the first few years of our marriage, we faced challenges that became a source of disunity in our relationship. It is difficult to have fun with someone you are not getting along with. However, Aaron and I made it a point to find ways to connect and enjoy life together despite our problems. We still took drives; there was just a little more silence back then. We explored antique shops, we went to the movies, and we chatted in bed. We enjoyed what we were doing even if we were experiencing hard circumstances within our relationship. We also found moments to make each other laugh by being quirky, like when I would awkwardly dance by Aaron just to see if I could get him to smile. It wasn't always on our minds to enjoy life together or go out of our way to make each other laugh, especially when things between us were rocky, but the times that we did stood out to us, because the effort required to do so reflected the love for each other that was still in our hearts. Having fun together reaffirmed our hearts toward our marriage, giving us hope for better days.

Being intentional to make each other laugh, being silly together, touching each other, and doing things together that you love is a reminder to each other that marriage is not a business transaction. Marriage is not just a means to accomplish your goals; marriage is a journey, and it is important that you both enjoy it along the way. That means even enjoying each other when hard times come or when unity is fractured. Take the time to have more fun and show each other that you enjoy your marriage.

Stronger Together

Stronger Together

If you hope for God to use your marriage to impact the world, being supportive of each other is also key. The light flickering from a candle can be seen in the darkness, but how much more is illuminated in that darkness when two lights are placed side by side? The energy and light intensifies exponentially. You and your spouse are lights in this world, lights that shine brightly showing God's truth, love, and grace. The two of you serving God together will always make a greater impact than the two of you could make alone, striving for your own accomplishments and happiness.

As you pursue living out a marriage after God, and as you and your spouse embrace the extraordinary unity of marriage, you must never forget that the two of you with God are stronger together. You, your spouse, and God are the three strands that make up the cord, the three strands that are not quickly broken. The benefit of being bound together with God at the center of your marriage relationship is that He is your source of strength and power. As the apostle Peter reminds us, "His divine power has granted to us all things that pertain to life and godliness, through the knowledge of him who called us to his own glory and excellence" (2 Peter 1:3). It is through His power that you and your spouse are able to do all that He has called you to do. Not through your power and not through your spouse's power, but through God's mighty power your marriage has been granted all things that pertain to life and godliness.

The apostle Peter goes on to say, "For this very reason, make every effort to supplement your faith with virtue, and virtue with knowledge, and knowledge with self-control, and self-control with steadfastness, and steadfastness with godliness, and godliness with brotherly affection, and brotherly affection with love. For if these qualities are yours and are increasing, they keep you from being ineffective or unfruitful in the knowledge of our Lord Jesus Christ" (2 Peter 1:5–8).

No one wants to be ineffective or unfruitful! So, if you desire your marriage to be effective for the kingdom, you should practice all these things: virtue, knowledge, self-control, steadfastness, godliness, brotherly affection, and love. You should strive for these things and encourage your spouse to do so as well. As you and your spouse draw closer to each other and chase after God, you will reap the extraordinary blessing of being stronger together, equipped to fulfill every good work He has for you to do.

QUESTIONS FOR REFLECTION

1. What is one thing you can do to communicate more effectively as a couple?
2. What does having fun together look like in your marriage? What do you like to do together? Pick something you both enjoy and do it today.

Chapter 16

CHASING AFTER
GOD TOGETHER

As we drove to church one Sunday morning, our five-year-old son asked, "Mom, Dad, you know why Peter fell when he was walking on the water toward Jesus?" I glanced toward my wife who had a puzzled look on her face. We both wondered what stimulated this big thought of his. My wife turned around to acknowledge our son, but before she could answer his question, he fired back, "Because he took his eyes off Jesus! Right, Dad?" This question led us into a conversation with our son about the importance of keeping our eyes on Jesus, being close to Jesus, and not letting fear overwhelm us.

Peter was doing something extraordinary by walking out on the water toward Jesus. He was motivated by a desire to be close to Him. However, as Peter made his way toward Jesus, Matthew 14:30 says, "But when he saw the wind, he was afraid, and beginning to sink he cried out, "Lord, save me." As we drove to church that morning, my wife pointed out that Peter was in such close proximity to Jesus that when Peter began to sink in the water and cried out for help, Jesus reached out His hand and grabbed Peter. Then my wife shared with our son, and reminded all of us, the importance of being close to Jesus and that when we call out to Him, He will help us.

Even though Peter was afraid, he still experienced an extraordinary moment with his Savior. Although he was distracted by the circumstance of the wind, losing sight of what he was doing, the Lord graciously helped him and guided him back to the boat.

Jesus was the One who directed His disciples to get into the boat earlier that day. In Matthew 14:25 Jesus comes back to join His disciples in a miraculous way, by walking on the water. With the desire to walk in His will and His ways and in marriages that claim the name of Christ, we must never forget that our Lord and Savior is coming back for us, His bride, and He will do so in a miraculous way. While we are waiting for His return, we must let this knowledge of His testimony and second coming be the fuel that ignites in us an unquenchable fire to boldly chase after God's will for our marriages. The beautiful and imminent return of our King is the very thing that motivates us to move beyond our comfort into the amazing, extraordinary, powerful, world-changing "good works" that God has prepared for each one of us since before time began.

How incredibly empowering and encouraging is that?

Just before the risen Jesus ascended into heaven, He said, "All authority in heaven and on earth has been given to me. Go therefore and make disciples of all nations, baptizing them in the name of the Father and of the Son and of the Holy Spirit, teaching them to observe all that I have commanded you. And behold, I am with you always, to the end of the age" (Matthew 28:18–20).

Jesus gave us a job to spread His gospel around the world and to obey His every command. But that Great Commission came with a promise: He will be with us. Not only that, but someday He will return to us and take us to Himself (John 14:3).

God has entrusted you with tools, gifts, and resources with the command and holy expectation that you will invest them well, so that upon His return He can receive the profit and glory from your lives. Whether or not you believe you are qualified to fulfill this heavenly job doesn't matter, because the Creator Himself put in you the only One who is qualified, the Holy Spirit. You are enough, you are qualified, you are called because you are in Him and He is in you.

How comforting it is to know that you are not alone! Not only has God given you everything needed to accomplish the righteous tasks set before you, but He has given you His Spirit. You have received from Him the living, breathing, empowering Holy Spirit of God Himself quickening your dead body. By yourself you can do nothing to please the Creator of the universe, but with the Spirit you can be and do the very things that you could not do in your own strength.

In addition to His Holy Spirit, He has given you the gift of a spouse. Your relationship with your spouse is intimate and unique; no other earthly relationship can compare to it. Supporting one another, encouraging each other, and experiencing the extraordinary gift of oneness in marriage will build you up and affirm you so that you can continue to persevere through any circumstance. Having a spouse beside you is a gift, as you both point each other toward God whenever either of you are tempted to be afraid or insecure. You are not alone!

Furthermore, He has also blessed you with the security and

sharpening that comes only with fellowship in His body. This body is made up of many parts, and every part has been given gifts for the mutual uplifting and edification of the others. The body exists everywhere. The body is present and alive, a gift of life and of camaraderie. Whatever you are facing in your life, the good news is this: you are not alone!

We may have come to the end of our book, but by no means is this the end of yours. Your book, your story, the ministry that your marriage is equipped to bring to this world in whatever form or fashion, is just beginning. This is your call to arms, your challenge to rise up, your invitation to join the millions of Christian marriages around the world who are going to bring the message of the Savior to their children, friends, neighbors, and as He wills, even further.

It is time to say yes to God and let Him use your marriage in

It is time to say YES to God.

the mighty way He intended it to be used. It is time to surrender your money to be used not only to support your family's needs and the ministry work you have been invited to do but also to support the saints in their work for the gospel. It is time to let your home be a place not only for teaching your children the goodness of God and the truth of His Word but also of refuge for your neighbors and friends, a place of healing and love for those who are seeking the good news that is on display in your life. It is time to allow the natural talents God gave you to be used to bless others and point people to Him. It is time to allow your story, your experiences, and your testimony of Jesus saving you to impact the lives of others in every opportunity God gives you. It is time to say yes to Him.

We love the story of Peter walking on the water. One aspect of that story that always inspires us is how eager and motivated Peter is to be with Jesus. When he sees Jesus, he calls, "Command me to come to you on the water" (Matthew 14:28). Peter knew and respected the authority of Jesus Christ in his life. He submitted to the Lord's will, and he wanted to be directed by him. He also desired to be with Jesus wherever He was, even if that meant out on the open water. Peter didn't ask the Lord to meet him where he was—safe and dry in the boat. Rather, he asked Jesus to command him to come to where *He* was.

Our heart's desire is that you and your spouse would have this same reverence and submission in your relationship with the Lord. That you would be a husband and wife willing to ask God to call you out of the boat, to have courage to join Him when He does, and to walk in obedience to all that He commands you to do. That you would pursue closeness to Him and desire to be near to Him always. That you would chase after the extraordinary experiences God has for you, not for your glorification or fulfillment, but for the Lord's glorification and the fulfillment of His will.

Boldly chase after God. Don't look back, and you will never regret it. Everything you have is *from* God and is *for* God. So then, let everything you do be done in love and for the glory of God. This is God's will for your life. This is His heart for you and your marriage, and He will give you the strength to live it out. He deserves all the glory and honor and praise in and through your life. He deserves your devotion and adoration, because He is the only true God who made heaven and earth. He is your rescuer, and nothing you can do can earn what He freely gave to you in His Son, Jesus. But Jesus is the very reason that you can say yes to Him and submit your marriage to Him in service.

This is not a call to a life without trial or tribulation, but rather, to a life that expects it. Bear in mind that we live in a world that hates us for following Jesus, and we have a real spiritual enemy called the devil who hates us for the same reason. We also have our flesh that constantly opposes the Spirit. Knowing this, make sure you take the Word of God seriously when it tells you to walk in the Spirit so that you will not gratify the desires of the flesh. Put on the full armor of God so that you will be prepared for the attacks of the enemy and will be able to stand up under them. You and your spouse can be open-eyed about these dangers and stand strong as a marriage after God, together, in complete unity.

As Paul prayed for the Colossians, so we pray for you and your spouse that you would "be filled with the knowledge of his will in all spiritual wisdom and understanding, so as to walk in a manner worthy of the Lord, fully pleasing to him: bearing fruit in every good work and increasing in the knowledge of God" (Colossians 1:9–10). When you abide in the Lord and when you choose to walk in a manner worthy of His calling, you pave the way for others to follow God. As you choose holiness over happiness, your marriage will grow in maturity, able to bear the weight of abundant fruit, so that others can taste the goodness of the Lord through your life and marriage. As you make choices that lead to an increase in intimacy in your marriage and in the intimacy of knowing God, the will of the Father and the good works He has prepared for you will become clearer.

Chasing after the extraordinary marriage God has designed for you and your spouse can be terrifying. Like standing up in a boat, looking down at the raging water, and stepping in. Like sitting in a living room full of couples who are staring at you, taking a deep breath and then challenging them to consider what they can do to be builders for God's kingdom. Or navigating your children through the ups and downs of life, motivated by the truth that you are leaving a legacy of faith. Or talking to the woman who sits in your salon chair about the truth of what God thinks about her. Or adopting a child, starting that business, writing that book, practicing hospitality, or any other terrifying invitation God gives you to step out of the boat to join Him. Don't be afraid! God is whispering, "Come, and I will be with you." God is good, and He has good plans for your marriage. He will never leave you, nor forsake you! Chase after God and never stop saying yes to Him.

QUESTIONS FOR REFLECTION

1. What are you most afraid of when it comes to chasing after God's will together?
2. How does it help you to know that you have everything you need to accomplish God's purposes?
3. How might God be calling you to use your marriage for the building of His kingdom?

ACKNOWLEDGMENTS

First and foremost, we would like to thank God for His love and for sending His Son, Jesus, so we can be set free from sin and death. Thank You for Your holy Word, which directs our steps. And thank You for opening our eyes and hearts to Your powerful purpose of marriage. We love You, Lord!

Thank you, Matt and Lisa, for leading us by example in life, parenting, and marriage, and for showing us that God's Word is of utmost importance in our lives.

We would like to thank our local fellowship for constant support, accountability, and prayers as we journey through life, and especially through the season of writing this book.

To our dearest children, thank you for your patience with us during the long days and nights of working on this book. We pray that as you grow up and get married that this message blesses you as you pursue God's purposes for your own marriages.

To every marriage that has been a personal example to us of what it means to have a marriage after God, thank you. Your faithfulness in your own marriage has greatly impacted us in ours.

We would also like to thank all the husbands and wives who have participated in our online ministries and supported us throughout the years on social media. Your stories have been such an encouragement to our family along the way.

Thank you to all the "Movement Starters" who faithfully share this book with others and spread the *Marriage After God* message through word of mouth, by gifting copies of this book to friends and coworkers, by sharing their lives with their neighbors, and who are allowing God to use their own marriage for His glory.

Thank you, Stephanie, for believing in this book and for the excitement you have had all along the way! Your encouragement during the editing process made us feel special, that our message was validated, and overall, we have felt incredibly loved!

And finally, thank you to the Zondervan team not only for the opportunity to spread this message but also for believing in us to do so. We value the way you have trusted us and worked so well to make this book what it is. From the bottom of our hearts and to each one of you who had a hand in this publication, thank you!

DREAMING TOGETHER
CONVERSATION STARTERS

Dreaming together and communicating effectively are important components of building a marriage after God. To get you started on the journey of a marriage after God, here is a list of potential topics for your conversation together. Come prepared by choosing one or more of these topics for discussion and set a time to talk when you will not be disturbed. Take notes on what you've discussed, and end in prayer. But most of all, enjoy each other's company, perspective, vision, and wisdom.

PRESSING ISSUES

Is there a situation or opportunity or crisis that we need to talk through?

What might God be telling us in this situation?

DREAMS FOR OUR MARRIAGE

Evaluate your marriage in light of the seven marks of a marriage after God:

Does our marriage demonstrate oneness? Are we unified?

Does our marriage demonstrate submission? Do we listen to each other and support each other?

Is our marriage biblical? Are we walking with God individually and as a couple?

Is our marriage sacrificial? In what ways might God be asking us to make sacrifices in our marriage?

Is our marriage transparent? Do we openly share our thoughts and feelings without fear?

Is our marriage intimate? Do we pursue and enjoy sexual intimacy?

Is our marriage an example to others of God's love? Can we honestly encourage others to follow our example?

DREAMS FOR OUR FAMILY

How is God calling us to build our family?

What as parents do we do well? Where can we do better?

How can we best parent each of our children in light of their ages, personalities, and interests? How can we disciple them to grow and mature in their knowledge of God?

DREAMS FOR OUR PROFESSION

What work, either paid or unpaid, is God calling us to do?

How does our work impact our marriage and our family?

How might we use our work to build God's kingdom?

DREAMS FOR OUR FINANCES

What financial goal(s) do we need to pursue next? How can we begin to live a debt-free lifestyle?

How might God want us to use our finances to bless the church?

How might God want us to use our finances to bless the world and spread the gospel?

DREAMS FOR OUR SPIRITUAL LIFE

Are we each reading and studying the Word daily?

Are we participating in true fellowship with other believers?

Take inventory of your marriage tool belt:

What experiences have we had that God might want to use?

What is our testimony, both individually and as a couple, and how might God want to use it?

What are our talents and gifts, and how might they be used to build God's kingdom?

What resources do we have and how does God desire us to use them for His purposes?

DREAMS ABOUT THE FUTURE

Where do we want to be in five years?

Where do we want to be in ten years?

Where do we want to be in twenty-five years?

What vision do we have for the future?

What goals do we have, and what tasks will help us to achieve those goals?

Remember: dreaming together is a fun, intimate experience where hope for the future stimulates perseverance for today!

GO DEEPER WITH

more encouraging and inspirational marriage
resources by Aaron & Jennifer Smith

Please Visit

MARRIAGEAFTERGOD.COM/godeeper

Check out these 30-day
marriage devotionals

Also look for the
prayer books

WOULD YOU LIKE MORE?
Check out the Marriage After God weekly podcast by the authors!

Visit
MARRIAGEAFTERGOD.COM/podcast

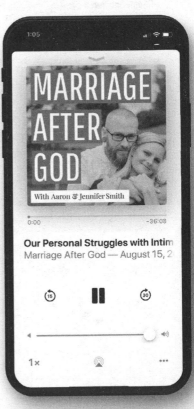